HIGHER

EDUCATION

DOLLARS AND

SENSE

The College Board

100 YEARS

HIGHER

EDUCATION

DOLLARS AND

SENSE

A FRAMEWORK FOR CAMPUS DISCUSSIONS

SANDY BAUM

COLLEGE ENTRANCE EXAMINATION BOARD
NEW YORK, 2001

The College Board is a national nonprofit membership association dedicated to preparing, inspiring, and connecting students to college and opportunity. Founded in 1900, the association is composed of more than 3,900 schools, colleges, universities, and other educational organizations. Each year, the College Board serves over three million students and their parents, 22,000 high schools, and 3,500 colleges through major programs and services in college admission, guidance, assessment, financial aid, enrollment, and teaching and learning. Among its best-known programs are the SAT®, the PSAT/NMSQT™, the Advanced Placement Program® (AP®), and Pacesetter®. The College Board is committed to the principles of equity and excellence, and that commitment is embodied in all of its programs, services, activities, and concerns.

In memory of
Werner A. Baum (1923 – 1999),
who taught me much of what I know and love
about higher education

CONTENTS

ACKNOWLEDGMENTS

Many of my friends and colleagues made valuable contributions to this work. My experiences at Skidmore College provided a considerable amount of the background for this project, which grew out of a conversation with Michael McPherson. Jim Chansky, Eban Goodstein, Sarah Goodwin, Don Hossler, Tim Koechlin, Kathleen Little, Bruce Mallette, Pat Oles, Morton Schapiro, and Jamienne Studley read drafts and made very helpful suggestions. Any errors or omissions remaining are entirely my own.

Introduction

The relationships among employees at colleges and universities are different from those in any other type of enterprise. Administrators' responsibility for day-to-day operations and for many fundamental decisions is quite similar to the responsibility of management in many other organizations, and the administration's accountability to the Board of Trustees or other oversight bodies is similar to management's responsibility to corporate boards. But the type of shared governance in which faculty participate on most campuses contrasts starkly with other organizational structures.

This shared governance, which gives faculty much more input into key decisions than most employees elsewhere have, provides a critical form of empowerment without which faculty jobs would be considerably less appealing to many of the talented people who now choose this occupation. The engagement of faculty in decisions about institutional priorities, curricular design, and personnel matters is usually regarded as a prerequisite for creating an intellectual and educational community that maximizes the contributions of all of its members.

Yet shared governance creates considerable tension on many campuses. Faculty may complain that their voice—the voice with the greatest understanding of the academic mission—is not adequately heard. Administrators may feel beleaguered by the many layers of committee deliberations and faculty agreements required to move agendas forward. Oversight bodies may become impatient with the apparent inefficiency of the campus governance process compared to the more hierarchical systems familiar to the corporate world and may call for the redesign of college governance, with a higher priority placed on speed and efficiency.

This monograph is intended to strengthen the system of shared governance by providing the constituencies involved with some common terminology and by encouraging all interested individuals to analyze higher education institutions more carefully. The economic perspective on which this discussion is based does not lead to particular conclusions about the problems facing academic institutions today, but it does frame questions in ways that may be new to some readers. It focuses attention on the reality of limited resources and the necessity of making choices. It highlights ways in which colleges and universities differ dramatically from for-profit business because of their unique missions, but it also allows some basic concepts familiar to business people to be applied to the analysis of higher education finance.

Readers who have been engaged in financial deliberations on campus will find much of the material in the beginning chapters to be a review. In order to bring even those people with no background in economics or campus budgeting into the conversation, the text provides very basic explanations of the relevant concepts. Chapter 1 provides background on the economic and demographic trends that create a context for understanding the current dilemmas faced by individual institutions. The focus of Chapter 2 is on basic economic concepts that can provide a foundation for common vocabulary, in addition to furthering understanding of the economic realities underpinning educational institutions. Many of the ideas found here will be familiar to those who have studied economics. Chapter 3 explains some of the basic concepts of college and university finance. Chapter 4 is the core, tackling some controversial campus issues, and Chapter 5 contains some questions that may be used as a starting point for conversations on campus. The relationship between an academic institution and a business, and the issues of compensation, tenure, and financial aid strategies are all analyzed using the economic concepts and reasoning introduced earlier. The goal is not to cover all of the key issues, but to provide a few examples of the way in which controversial issues might be analyzed to provide a stronger foundation for campus debate. The intention is not to move people towards a particular perspective or to create consensus on difficult issues. Rather, the purpose is to help faculty, administrators, and members of governing boards think in new ways about problems with which they are grappling and facilitate a dialogue giving voice to a variety of perspectives.

Parts of the discussion in this monograph may seem more relevant for private colleges and universities than on public campuses, where there is less room for discretion in the allocation of resources. People at four-year institutions with an established community of long-term, full-time faculty are most likely to be engaged with the issues discussed here. However, despite their differences, all institutions must grapple with the difficulty of pursuing the educational mission while maintaining fiscal stability. The concepts and principles contained in the following chapters should be useful for anyone faced with the reality of required trade-offs in an educational environment.

While there is considerable variation across campuses, at all colleges and universities the decision-making process differs significantly from standard business practices. A number of constituencies, all of whom share the basic goal of creating and maintaining a positive educational environment, have a role in the process. These constituencies, and the individuals who compose them, are likely to have quite different priorities. Faculty members may have curricular innovation or faculty compensation at the top of their lists, while admission staff are more concerned about improving the external image of the institution and financial officers must be actively engaged in searching for ways to hold down total expenditures. No amount of understanding of college financing, of common vocabulary or of constructive exchange of ideas will create a complete consensus on campus priorities, even among rational people who share the same basic goal. But successful shared governance does not require that all priorities be shared or that consensus be reached on all decisions. It does require that everyone be open to thinking in new ways and to engaging with the language and the values of others who share the goal of perpetuating and strengthening the mission of our educational institutions.

The Changing Environment of Colleges and Universities

I t is no accident that the 1990s brought tensions surrounding financing issues to the surface on college campuses. A variety of trends in the external environment have combined to make it impossible for colleges and universities to continue to expand and strengthen academic programs without explicit regard for financial constraints. An understanding of some of the characteristics of the changing context in which faculty, administrators, and higher education oversight bodies are functioning can facilitate constructive participation in campus debates.

The most obvious pressure has come from rapidly rising college costs combined with declining ability and willingness to pay on the part of many students and families, all of which has led to increased public scrutiny and criticism of higher education institutions. In addition, demographic trends and changing patterns of college enrollment have created a challenging climate for higher education.

The Rising Price of a College Education

In 2000–2001, average tuition and fees at four-year private colleges were $16,332, increasing from $3,617 in 1980-81 and $9,391 in 1990-91. There was, of course, a considerable amount of inflation throughout the economy over this 20-year period, but the real increase—in constant-value dollars—was 68 percent in the 1980s and 35 percent in the 1990s, or 127 percent over the two decades. In the public sector, where about 80 percent of undergraduates are enrolled, average tuition and fees at four-year public colleges and universities increased from $804 in 1980-81 to $1,809 in 1990-91 and $3,510 in 2000–2001. The inflation-adjusted increase was 46 percent in the 1980s and 51 percent in the 1990s, or 119 percent over the two decades.[1]

Examining this 20-year time period may obscure the extreme nature of the recent problems. In 1981–1982, the inflation-adjusted price tag on a private college education was actually slightly lower than it had been a decade earlier, and the real increase in the public sector in the 1970s totaled only 6 percent. It was during the 1980s that the trend changed. Table 1 shows the increases in average tuition and fees in the

1. The College Board, *Trends in College Pricing, 2000* (Washington, D.C.: The College Board, 2000), p. 7.

Table 1. Changes in Tuition and Fees at Four-Year Colleges and Universities, 1975–2001.						
	Private 4-year			**Public 4-year**		
	Tuition & fees (current dollars)	Tuition & fees (2000 dollars)	5-year inflation adjusted increase	Tuition & fees (current dollars)	Tuition & fees (2000 dollars)	5-year inflation adjusted increase
1975-76	$2,272	$7,071		$433	$1,348	
1980-81	$3,617	$7,207	2%	$804	$1,602	19%
1985-86	$5,418	$8,594	19%	$1,242	$1,970	23%
1990-91	$9,391	$12,104	41%	$1,809	$2,332	18%
1995-96	$12,432	$13,888	15%	$2,860	$3,195	37%
2000-01	$16,332	$16,332	18%	$3,510	$3,510	10%

Source: The College Board, *Trends in College Pricing, 2000.*

private and public sectors by five-year time periods from 1975-76 to 2000–2001. In private colleges and universities the most rapid increase in prices was in the middle and late 1980s. The growth rate of public sector prices peaked in the early to middle 1990s. Even with the more recent slowing in tuition growth in both sectors, the cost of attendance continues to rise at rates that would have been unimaginable as recently as the early 1970s.

Family Incomes

Given the rise in the price of a college education relative to the prices of other goods and services, it should not be a surprise that families are suffering diminishing ability to pay because their incomes are not keeping pace. Because of the dramatic differences in the income patterns of different segments of the population in recent decades, it is difficult to make general statements without distorting the real situations of many families. However, a few basic facts are useful.

Inflation-adjusted median family income in the United States rose less than 9 percent between 1980 and 1997 — a period when average tuition at private colleges rose 102 percent in real terms and average tuition at public colleges rose 107 percent. In 1997, the average private college tuition of $13,664 constituted 29 percent of the $46,754 median income for white families. For black and Hispanic families, the tuition was 48 percent of median family income. These figures exaggerate the affordability problem somewhat, since families headed by individuals between the ages of 45 and 54 — those most likely to have college-age children — tend to earn about 25 percent more than families in the overall population. Moreover, many students receive some form of financial aid and pay net prices significantly lower than the sticker prices cited here. Nonetheless, the strain on the typical family budget is clear.

For many people on four-year college campuses, it is difficult to maintain a realistic perspective on what is typical in the United States. In 1997, only 23 percent of families had incomes as high as $75,000.[2] It is hard to imagine that many of the other 77 percent of families face the prospect of financing college for one or more children with equanimity.

2. U.S. Census Bureau, *Statistical Abstract of the United States 1999* (Washington D.C.: U.S. Government Printing Office, 1999), Table 749.

Changes in the distribution of income among American families have made college financing even more of a stretch for a broad segment of the population. In 1970, the top 5 percent of families in the U.S. had 16 percent of total family income. By 1997, this group (with incomes above $137,000) had 21 percent of total income. Both low- and middle-income families suffered in relative terms, with the share of the bottom 20 percent falling from 5.4 to 4.6 percent between 1970 and 1997, and the share of the middle fifth declining from 18 to 15 percent. Defining the middle more broadly, the share of the middle 60 percent of families fell from 54 to 47 percent of total income.[3] The distribution of household wealth is even more skewed.

For those near the top of the income distribution, the sticker price of college has not become less affordable in any meaningful sense. The average cost of attendance at private four-year colleges has ranged between 12 and 15 percent of income over the last 30-year period for the top fifth of families. The less affluent have been less fortunate in this regard. For the lowest-income families, the jump was from 91 percent in 1971, and 84 percent in 1979, to 166 percent in 2000–2001.[4]

Increased inequality helps to explain the strain middle-income families are feeling. For a few families at the top of the scale, even the cost of attending the most expensive private colleges is quite manageable. But for most families, college affordability is a very real issue.

Student Aid

Families and students do not, of course, pay the entire cost of higher education themselves. Tuition and fees represent only about one-third of the cost of producing education at public institutions, with most of the remainder a subsidy from state governments. Even at private colleges and universities, virtually no students pay the full cost of their education. Tuition covers an average of about three-quarters of costs while institutional subsidies, funded largely by endowment income and annual giving, average over $5,000 per student.[5]

Beyond these general subsidies, federal and state governments, as well as institutions themselves, provide significant amounts of financial aid to students. In 1999–2000, there was over $68 billion in combined federal, state, and institutional aid available to postsecondary students.[6] Almost three-quarters of these dollars came from the federal government and close to 20 percent came from nongovernmental sources, primarily institutions.

Understanding the role of these resources is not possible without taking the composition of these funds into consideration. While colleges and universities tend to provide their aid to students in the form of grants, three-quarters of the federal government's aid comes in the form of loans to students. Overall, almost 60 percent of student aid dollars are in the form of loans.[7]

---

3. Ibid., Table 751.
4. The College Board, *Trends in College Pricing 2000*, p. 15.
5. National Commission on the Cost of Higher Education, *Straight Talk About College Costs and Prices* (Washington, D.C.: National Commission on the Cost of Higher Education, 1998) p. 8.
6. The College Board, *Trends in Student Aid 2000*
7. Ibid., p.12.

This fact is important for understanding student ability and willingness to pay. While the funds are available to most students, many can finance their educations only by borrowing significant amounts of money. The need to borrow may limit access for some students and certainly creates a burden for many. But borrowing is a quite reasonable means of financing higher education. College is an investment that pays off over a lifetime, both in terms of significant income premiums and in terms of other aspects of the quality of life. Nonetheless, concerns over the limits on student and family willingness to borrow increase the pressure on states and institutions to keep tuition increases in check.

Loans have not always constituted such a large part of available student aid. At the beginning of the 1980s, before the tuition spiral began, loans were slightly over 40 percent of aid dollars. By 1987, this figure had increased to 52 percent. After dipping slightly for a few years, the loan/grant ratio rose significantly between 1992 and 1996. Most of the explanation for this recent phenomenon is that federal loans have become much more widely available. Grant aid increased 54 percent in inflation-adjusted terms between 1989 and 1999, while loans rose by 125 percent.[8] Federal grant aid rose only about 18 percent in real terms. Although still a relatively small fraction of the total, state grants helped to compensate, growing about 58 percent in real terms. Institutionally funded grants grew over 100 percent,[9] putting pressure on many college budgets.

In summary, while federal grant aid has not grown nearly fast enough in the last decade to keep up with the rising cost of attending college, total grant aid has risen more rapidly, largely because institutions have devoted larger portions of their operating budgets to student grants. The division of institutional aid between need-based funding and grants designed to compete for desirable students has shifted measurably towards the latter. Nonetheless, had schools not increased their aid budgets, access and choice for low-income students would have been significantly reduced and private colleges and universities would have less diverse student bodies. (See the discussion of student aid in Chapter 4 for more detailed analysis of this issue.)

Overall, the growth in aid dollars has outstripped the growth in tuition and fees, but loans have become an increasingly important form of financing. For families and students these trends increase the burden of the growing gap between college costs and incomes. For colleges and universities, they intensify the strain on both the revenue and the expenditure sides of the budget.

The College Population

Despite these financial difficulties, the demand for a college education remains strong. College enrollments skyrocketed between 1965 and 1980. In the public sector, the number of students grew from about 4 million to 9.5 million over this 15-year period. The change in the private sector was much less dramatic, increasing from 2 million to 2.6 million. Total enrollment leveled off in the 1980s as the number of people of traditional college age declined—and the

---

8. Ibid., p.12.
9. Ibid., p.7.

cost of attending college skyrocketed. After a slight decline in the early 1990s, enrollments are projected to increase relatively rapidly over the coming decade.[10]

Overall enrollment projections and the changing characteristics of student bodies can best be understood in the context of a general picture of the changing demographics of the United States. Both the characteristics of the U.S. population and shifting college enrollment patterns within demographic groups have contributed to major changes in the demographic composition of the college-going population over the last two decades.

The decline in the number of college-aged people in the United States throughout the 1980s and into the middle of the 1990s created considerable pressure on colleges and universities trying to fill the spaces they had created to meet the increasing enrollments of the 1970s. The number of 15- to 19-year-olds actually fell between 1980 and 1992. Since then the trend has been reversed, but the number is still significantly below what it was 20 years ago.[11] It is good news for colleges that the danger from this particular trend is past. Current projections suggest that the number of 18- to 24-year olds will increase by about 20 percent between now and 2025.[12]

In 1970, 48 percent of 18- and 19-year-olds, 32 percent of 20-and 21-year-olds, and 15 percent of 22- to 24-year-olds were enrolled in school. By 1993, those percentages had risen to 62 percent, 43 percent, and 24 percent.[13] These increasing enrollment rates allowed colleges to survive the decrease in the number of traditional college-age Americans over the 1980s, and it is fortuitous that the leveling off of enrollment rates in the last few years coincides with renewed growth in the relevant age range.

The enrollment patterns of different groups within the population show considerable variation. Gender differences, for example, are striking. While the percentage of the U.S. population that is female has increased slowly over time—from 49 percent in 1920 to 50 percent in 1950 and 51 percent in 1998[14]—differential college attendance rates have caused a more dramatic gender imbalance on campuses. In 1970, 49 percent of women who had graduated from high school in the preceding 12 months were enrolled in college, compared to 55 percent of men. By 1998, 69 percent of the women and only 62 percent of the men were enrolled.[15]

People from different racial and ethnic backgrounds also have significantly different college attendance patterns. Although college attendance rates have risen dramatically in recent decades, the changing ethnic composition of the population promises to present continuing challenges to college admission officials, since the groups that historically have the highest enrollment rates are becoming a smaller portion of the U.S. population.

Table 2 shows higher education enrollment rates by race/ethnicity since 1976 for individuals ages 18 to 24. Among people of traditional college age, whites are much more likely than African Americans or people of Hispanic origin to be

10. National Center for Education Statistics, *Digest of Education Statistics, 1999* (Washington D.C.: U.S. Department of Education, 1999), p. 196.
11. U.S. Census Bureau, op.cit., Table 14.
12. Ibid., Table 17.
13. National Center for Education Statistics, op. cit., Table 177.
14. U.S. Census Bureau, op.cit., Table 13.
15. National Center for Education Statistics, op.cit., Table 187.

Table 2. Enrollment Rates by Race/Ethnicity: Individuals Age 18 to 24.

Year	White	Black	Hispanic	Total Enrollment Rate
1970	27%	16%	NA	26%
1980	27%	19%	16%	26%
1990	35%	25%	16%	32%
1998	41%	30%	20%	37%

Source: National Center for Education Statistics, *Digest of Education Statistics, 1999*, Table 189.

enrolled in higher education. Despite the increasing enrollment rates for minority groups, the gap between college attendance rates of whites and the rest of the population is growing.

The groups with lower enrollment rates constitute an increasing proportion of the population. In 1950, 89 percent of the population was white. This proportion declined slowly to 88 percent in 1970, but reached 83 percent in 1995 and is projected to fall to 78 percent by the year 2025. Over the same period of time, African Americans, who constituted 10 percent of the population in 1950, have grown to 13 percent and will be 14 percent of the population by 2025. The Hispanic population, about 6 percent in 1980 when the Census started counting, accounts for most of the growth in groups with relatively low enrollment rates, now constituting 11 percent of the population and expected to grow to 18 percent by 2025.[16]

Enrollment rates also differ significantly by family income levels. Among 1992 high school graduates, the average person from the highest 20 percent of the income distribution was 34 percentage points more likely than the average person from the lowest quintile to go to college. Controlling for differences in test scores reduces this differential, but it remains 21 percentage points. Among students who scored in the top 25 percent of test takers, 94 percent enrolled in college. However, those at the top of the income distribution were still 14 percentage points more likely than those at the bottom with the same high test scores to go to college.[17] Similar results emerge if high school class rank is used to identify high-ability students.

If the gap between enrollment rates of whites and non-whites and between lower- and higher-income Americans does not narrow, many colleges and universities will find that changing demographics and increasing inequality will continue to exacerbate their financial difficulties.

The trends described above have not and will not affect all campuses in the same way. For public institutions, state funding remains the central issue, while private institutions are much more tuition dependent. Urban universities and states with large concentrations of immigrants are more likely to feel the changing ethnic composition of the college-age population than are others. But on every campus, some combination of cost pressures and revenue constraints is likely to keep choices forced by fiscal constraints at the center of campus controversies for the foreseeable future.

---

16. Ibid., p. 14.
17. Tom Kane, *The Price of Admission: Rethinking How Americans Pay for College* (Washington D.C.: The Brookings Institution, 1999), pp. 98+.

Basic Economic Concepts and College Financing

In order to carry on a constructive conversation about campus finances and their relationship to the mission of the educational institution, we need to have a common vocabulary. Many terms that crop up in campus debates are laden with connotations unappealing to one constituency or another. For example, faculty who hear trustees or regents discussing the *demand for the product* at their institution are quite likely to fear that those using this terminology are failing to focus on the unique nature of the services faculty provide. Administrators responsible for institutional finance may bristle when they hear faculty argue that attempts to measure their output and increase their productivity suggest a serious misunderstanding of their work.

Perhaps more familiarity with economic terminology will allow those whose primary responsibility lies in shaping educational opportunities for students to participate in financial conversations. It may also allow those with responsibility for the bottom line to more clearly distinguish between the forces shaping higher education finance and those at work in for-profit markets for goods and services.

The first step in this process is to define economic concepts that have broad applicability, but have particular meaning in the context of college and university finance.

Opportunity Cost

Perhaps the single most important concept all participants in the college financing debate must understand and internalize is that of trade-offs. On some level, we all know that we can't have everything we want and that in order to get some of the things that are important to us, we must sacrifice other good things. But this reality is too frequently forgotten when we are dealing with the large dollar amounts that appear in institutional budgets and attempting to balance the legitimate interests of a variety of groups.

The *opportunity cost* of a purchase or a decision is the value of the best foregone opportunity. We tend to define the cost of attending college as the sum of the tuition, room, and board bills. But in fact, the cost is much higher. Students who devote themselves to their studies are foregoing the opportunity to participate more fully in the labor market. The opportunity cost of their time is part of the full cost of attending college. The cost of full-time attendance at an institution where tuition, room, and board add up to $25,000 a year is $25,000 plus the wages the student could have received for full-time labor force participation. In other words, the $1,000 a week price tag creating a sensation on the cover of *Newsweek*[1] a few years ago was a $300 to $400 understatement.[2]

> **Opportunity cost**: The value of the best alternative foregone in making any choice.

Opportunity cost is a useful concept in many campus discussions. We must, for example, decide how frequently to replace campus computers. Most of us agree that up-to-date technology is a good thing. Most of us would rather have a new computer than an old one. We would rather have VCRs and computer facilities in every classroom than have to reserve one of a few portable pieces of equipment in advance and have it delivered to the classroom. Most of us believe it is good to have dorm rooms wired for computer networking. But the debate should not be over whether these things are *good* or not. The question is what we will be giving up in exchange. Are we willing to have lower salary increases to pay for this level of technology? Are we willing to raise tuition and limit access to our institutions? Are we willing to forgo the new gymnasium?

The bottom line is that arguments that are simply about why a proposed innovation would be a good thing ignore reality. The debate must include opportunity cost, posing the question of why the benefit from the addition of the proposed program or activity will be greater than the cost of losing something we are now doing or of foregoing an alternative innovation.

Supply

Anyone who has taken an introductory economics course knows that the concepts of supply and demand are fundamental to almost any discussion of economic issues. In the present context, we might focus on the supply of and demand for seats in college classrooms, the supply of and demand for professional journals for the library, or the supply of and demand for computer scientists in the faculty labor market.

First, the basics. The graph in Figure 1 relates the price of a seller's product to the quantity of the product the seller is willing to supply over a given period of time. The upward sloping curve suggests that as the price sellers can command for their product increases, they are willing to supply larger quantities. *Supply curves* are frequently assumed to look this way, at least in the short run, primarily because of the capacity constraints created by any given level of physical plant and equipment.

The cost of producing additional units of output tends to increase as output levels increase. Suppliers may hire more workers to produce more, but these workers have limited space and a limited amount of equipment with which to work, so they can't contribute as much as workers added earlier. Only rising prices can make it profit-maximizing to incur these costs. Another reason suppliers may be willing to produce larger quantities at higher prices, as suggested by an upward sloping supply curve, is

---

1. *Newsweek*, Cover, April 29, 1996.
2. In 1996, the average male high school graduate between the age of 18 and 24 working year-round full-time earned $18,800. For females, the figure was $15,200. (U.S. Census Bureau, op.cit., p.476)

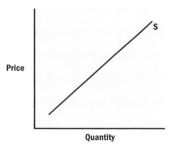

Figure 1: *Upward Sloping Supply Curve:* As the price increases, the quantity supplied increases. At higher tuition levels, some colleges will choose to enroll more students.

that as the price rises, alternative uses of resources become relatively less appealing.

If colleges have upward sloping supply curves for classroom seats, they will seek to increase the size of their student bodies only if the tuition they can charge increases. However, there are a variety of reasons why some colleges might be willing to increase the size of their student bodies without raising their prices. As is the case for any supplier, the cost conditions at any particular institution will determine the shape of its supply curve.

The supply curve may be horizontal over some range, as illustrated in Figure 2. This is the supply curve for a college that is willing to enroll a significantly higher number of students without raising its price. This would be the case if the cost of educating additional students is relatively low and essentially constant, as it would be for schools with excess capacity.

On the other hand, if they are operating at capacity, colleges may not be able to increase the number of spaces supplied without undertaking considerable capital investment and hiring additional personnel. It might be necessary to build new classrooms or residence halls, for example. This would be reflected in a vertical supply curve, as illustrated in Figure 3, at least in the short run. Increasing tuition levels would not lead these colleges to enroll more students, given the existing facilities.

An additional complication is the reality that colleges and universities are not profit-maximizing enterprises. Even if more students would generate additional revenues without significantly increasing costs, institutions may determine that increasing the size of the student body would require lowering admission standards or altering the student experience and thus diminishing the quality of their product. In this case, they may arbitrarily create a vertical supply curve, placing a limit on the number of places they are willing to supply, regardless of how much potential students are willing to pay and of the short-run cost of accommodating them.

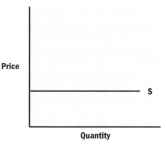

Figure 2: *Horizontal Supply Curve:* The quantity supplied can be increased without the price rising. Some colleges may have excess capacity and be willing to enroll additional students without raising tuition levels.

BASIC ECONOMIC CONCEPTS AND COLLEGE FINANCING

Figure 3: *Vertical Supply Curve:* The quantity supplied will not increase regardless of what happens to price. Some colleges may be operating at capacity and be unable to accommodate additional students even at higher tuition levels.

Some of the unique characteristics of education may cause institutions to find that as they enroll more students, incremental costs rise even though there are no capacity constraints. This might occur because of variation in the characteristics of the students. Unlike other products, education is not something customers can purchase and take away, with the producer's involvement ending once payment is made. The characteristics of the students can significantly affect the resources required for the institution to provide an adequate education. If colleges fill their beds by accepting students with limited academic preparation, with severe learning disabilities, or with other characteristics that make it more difficult for them to succeed, the incremental cost of educating these students will be higher and tuition may have to increase to cover these costs. The interdependency of student quality and cost of education may create an upward sloping supply curve, reflecting the higher costs of serving additional students, even when there is considerable excess capacity.

Institutions in different situations will find themselves with dramatically different supply schedules. A small number of colleges and universities in this country may have more qualified applicants willing to pay the full price than they can reasonably accommodate. They are on the vertical segment of their supply curves. In contrast, an increasing number of institutions are having considerable difficulty attracting enough students with enough ability to pay to operate anywhere near capacity. For these schools, the relevant supply curve is probably close to horizontal. If qualified students with the requisite funds were to appear, the schools would expand their enrollments without raising prices. Normally, only as they approach capacity would they find incremental costs of additional students increasing. The supply curve is horizontal when the college is operating far below capacity and then gradually becomes vertical as it reaches capacity, or as its costs of educating additional students rise for some other reason (Figure 4).

Figure 4: *Supply Curve with Changing Slope:* At low levels of output, the quantity can increase with no upward pressure on price, but as capacity is approached, quantity only increases if price also increases. Most colleges will face capacity constraints at some level of enrollment, but many may now be operating below this level.

Demand

A basic rule of economics is that the quantity of goods and services people choose to buy depends on prices. When apples are expensive, people may choose to buy fewer apples and more oranges. As the price of apples falls, more people will pay attention to the maxim that an apple a day keeps the doctor away.

There are downward sloping *demand curves* for most goods and services, including higher education. That is, as the price increases, quantity demanded decreases. As prices go up, some people decide going to college is not worth it after all. Although many students are willing to pay higher prices for institutions they perceive as providing higher quality education, low-cost institutions attract other students, who would never consider paying the prices charged by expensive private colleges. The slope of the demand curve reveals how much the quantity demanded changes when the price changes. A steep demand curve (Figure 5a) reflects small responses to changes in price, while a flatter curve indicates larger increases in the quantity demanded as the price falls (Figure 5b).

When a demand curve relating price and quantity is drawn, many factors have to be assumed to remain constant. These include the size of the population, consumers' preferences, income levels, the distribution of income, and the prices of goods and services that might be substitutes or complements (goods that are consumed together with the goods in question). If any of these factors change, the whole demand curve will shift.

For example, an increase in the population of recent high school graduates in the Northeast may mean that at any possible price, the number of students interested in attending Skidmore, a private liberal arts college in New York, will be higher. If general skepticism about the value of a liberal arts education increases, the opposite will occur—the demand curve will shift in as illustrated in Figure 6. In a recession, when incomes are generally lower, fewer people will be able to pay Skidmore's price. This will also be the case if inequality in the distribution of income increases. As income becomes much more concentrated at the top, while a small minority can easily pay for a private college education, it is out of reach for a greater proportion of high school graduates unless financial aid increases enough to compensate for declining incomes.

If private college prices remain constant, but tuition at the state university increases, the demand for private college education is likely to increase. More people will be willing to pay Skidmore's price, not because they are responding to changes in

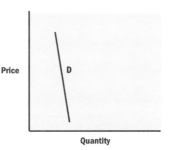

Figure 5a: *Steep Demand Curve:* Quantity demanded is not very sensitive to price changes. Some groups of students are unlikely to significantly alter their enrollment patterns in response to small changes in tuition levels.

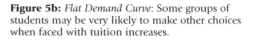

Figure 5b: *Flat Demand Curve*: Some groups of students may be very likely to make other choices when faced with tuition increases.

Skidmore's price or because their preferences have changed, but because the price of a close substitute—a reasonable alternative to Skidmore—has increased. On the other hand, when complementary goods become more expensive, the demand for a private Northeastern college education will decline. If, for example, students from other parts of the country are affected by a dramatic increase in airfares or if personal computers become a necessity for college students, the college's demand curve will shift in.

It is important to note that demand is a function both of people's preferences and of their available amount of money. In other words, both willingness to pay and ability to pay matter. Standard economic discussions of demand tend to focus on willingness to pay. People are willing to pay higher prices for the first pizza they buy each week, when they crave pizza, than for the tenth, when they are getting bored eating too much of the same thing. In the jargon of economic analysis, the marginal utility of pizza declines as the consumer has more and more of it in a given time period. The amount of satisfaction delivered by the first pizza is greater than the amount of satisfaction delivered by the tenth, and it is this added satisfaction that determines willingness to pay.

However, the demand curve doesn't just measure how much people want something. It measures effective demand, or demand backed up by dollars. A classic example is the comparison of the amount a poor man is willing to pay for milk for his baby to the amount a wealthy man is willing to pay for milk for his cat. Does the wealthy man care more about his cat than the poor man cares about his baby? Does he get more satisfaction from the milk? Or is the poor man simply unable to come up with the cash to pay for the milk?

The lesson here is that the demand curve necessarily represents willingness to pay combined with ability to pay. If the market is in equilibrium and everyone willing to pay the price is getting the quantity of milk they demand, this does not mean that everyone has what they need, that everyone is happy, or that society should feel comfortable with the outcome.

Figure 6: *Shift in Demand*: A decrease in demand for college may occur because of declining ability to pay caused by a recession or by increased income inequality.

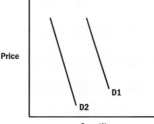

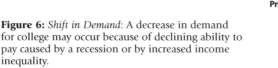

College officials, particularly those in the financial aid office, are increasingly aware of the distinction between ability to pay and willingness to pay. The need-based financial aid system is designed to ameliorate the problem illustrated by the milk example. The concept of need-based aid rests on the premise that people interested in attending college and able to benefit from the opportunity should have access, regardless of their ability to pay. Need-based financial aid constitutes an attempt to shift the demand curve out by increasing the resources available to pay for college. (Another way of looking at the phenomenon is in terms of net price. Financial aid lowers the effective price and, at lower prices, more people are able to pay.)

Recently, people with sufficient resources to pay for college have become more resistant to paying. They are demanding financial aid in order to keep them from choosing less expensive alternatives. In other words, willingness to pay has come to the fore as an issue in the demand for higher education. Many colleges have responded by transferring some of their funds from need-based aid to aid based on academic qualifications or other personal characteristics that might affect willingness to pay.

Changing priorities and a declining willingness to sacrifice consumption of other goods and services appear to be shifting the demand curve for higher education in. However, as the enrollment data suggest, other factors are working in the opposite direction. One of these is the increasing earnings gap between those with and without a college education. In 1998, mean earnings for men with a bachelor's degree were $50,056 — 77 percent more than the average for male high school graduates. In 1980, the earnings premium for a college degree was only 52 percent.[3] As the wages of workers with only a high school education have fallen in recent years, going to college has looked like a better investment to more people.

The Interaction of Supply and Demand

It is the interaction of supply and demand in a market that determines where the price settles and what quantity is purchased. A useful example may be faculty labor markets. Economists have a variety of competing theories about the determination of wage levels. Several of them can provide some insight into the evaluation of relative salaries on campus, an issue discussed more fully in Chapter 4 on campus issues. However, the most basic notion, with which few economists would disagree, is that supply and demand contribute to wage differentials.

One reason why occupations that do not require special skills tend to command lower wages is that there are many people who can fill those positions. For any given level of demand, higher levels of supply put downward pressure on the wage, just as would be the case for the price of any other good or service. If three new pizza parlors open near campus, the price of pizza is likely to fall. However, if, at the same time, the campus dining hall gets an unsatisfactory rating from the health department, demand for off-campus food will rise, putting upward pressure on pizza prices. The resulting price will depend on the balance between the changes in supply and demand. Similarly, an increase in the number of students earning Ph.D.'s in English will put downward pressure on starting salaries. Increases in corporate spending on research

3. U.S. Department of Commerce, *Statistical Abstract of the United States, 1999,* Table 265; *1982-83,* Table 231.

and development may create additional jobs for scientists in private business, raising the salaries universities have to pay to attract them. In other words, the forces of supply and demand—not just a sense of equity—affect the campus salary structure.

The Gender Imbalance on College Campuses

In recent years, many colleges and universities have found more women than men enrolling at their institutions. In 1975, 35 percent of male high school graduates between the age of 18 and 21 were in college, compared to 32 percent of females. By 1997, the enrollment rate for men in this category had increased to 42 percent, but was now lower than the 48 percent of 18- to 21-year-old female high school graduates who were enrolled in college.[4] In other words, more young men and more young women are choosing to go to college, but the increase is significantly greater for women. How can the concepts of supply and demand augment our understanding of this difference in the behavior of men and women?

The demand curve shows the relationship between price and quantity. Tuition, room, and board have risen at the same rate for men and women. However, the total cost of attending college includes the *opportunity cost* in terms of foregone wages. Wages for men have been rising more slowly than wages for women. This means that the total cost of attending college has risen more slowly for men than for women. In other words, if the cost of college were the determining factor, male enrollment rates would be increasing more rapidly than female enrollment rates.

The explanation lies in rapid shifts in women's demand for college education. At any price that might be in effect, more women are choosing college now than was the case in the past. Women's demand for higher education has increased more rapidly than men's for several reasons. Women's wages have risen more rapidly than men's in occupations requiring a college education, causing the return to education to rise more for women than it has for men. However, changes in social norms appear to have had a greater effect. The more diverse roles and greater opportunities available to women have increased their college enrollments. More occupations are open to women and more women work outside the home than was the case a generation ago. As a result, the number of women willing to pay the price of education has risen more rapidly than the number of men willing to pay the price.

From the institutions' perspectives, this change looks like a decrease in the supply of male students relative to the supply of female students. For residential coeducational colleges, this gender imbalance creates problems. It is possible that the relative decline in the supply of male students would lead colleges to be willing to pay more for men than for women. It would be surprising if institutional aid funds were used to lower the dollar price for men in order to attract them, but it is possible that greater investment in athletic facilities, changes in academic programs, or some form of preference for men in the admission process is occurring in an effort to increase the supply of men choosing to enroll.

4. U.S. Census Bureau, Ibid., Table 304.

Price Sensitivity

Many colleges facing downward sloping demand curves are interested in knowing how much their enrollments are likely to decline if they raise their net tuition and fees. This question relates to the *elasticity of demand*. If demand is *elastic*, a small increase in price will lead to a relatively large decline in the quantity demanded. The demand for Bic pens is elastic because people can easily substitute other brands of pens. The demand for automobiles is elastic because a small percentage increase in price constitutes a large chunk of the average consumer's budget. In addition, consumers can fairly easily decide to keep their old cars for another year or two.

The demand for some other products is *inelastic*. This means that although there is probably a downward sloping demand curve, the quantity demanded is not very sensitive to changes in price. The demand for insulin is inelastic because it is a necessity for those who use it and there are no good substitutes. The demand for salt is inelastic because even if the price doubles or triples, consumers won't notice it much in their budgets.

> **Elasticity of demand**: The change in quantity demanded in response to a change in price. If demand is *elastic*, quantity demanded changes more than in proportion to the change in price. An increase in price will cause total revenue to decline, while a decrease in price will increase revenues.
>
> If demand is *inelastic*, quantity demanded changes less than in proportion to the change in price. An increase in price will cause total revenue to increase, while a decrease in price will decrease revenues.

The elasticity of demand for college is an important question both because it is a key element in access to educational opportunity and because it has a major impact on institutional revenues. Suppose net tuition (tuition minus institutionally-funded student grants) increases by 5 percent this year. If enrollments decline by exactly 5 percent, revenues will remain constant. If demand is inelastic and enrollments decline by less than 5 percent, total revenues will increase. But if demand is elastic and enrollment declines by more than 5 percent, total revenues will decrease as a result of the increase in tuition. While precise measures of elasticity are difficult to obtain, most of the available evidence suggests that the actual elasticity of demand for college education in general, as well as for particular institutions, is lower than much of the public discussion about the dangers of rising tuitions might suggest. As discussed in the preceding chapter, enrollments have remained strong in the face of a dip in the college-aged population during a period of rapidly rising tuition levels. However, choices among institutions do appear to be more sensitive to price differentials than was the case 20 years ago.

For some students, the decision is whether to enroll in college or to enter the labor market. Increases in public college tuition levels, and particularly in the cost of attending community colleges, can certainly discourage a significant number of potential students. But for many others, the real decision is about which type of institution to attend or which particular institution is most appealing. When tuition levels at private colleges rise, more people are likely to choose public colleges. When tuition levels at four-year institutions rise, more people are likely to choose two-year colleges. If Princeton lowers the price it charges middle-class homeowners, they may attract some students who might otherwise have gone to Harvard. If the University of Rochester gives a $5,000 discount to New York State residents, they will attract some students who might otherwise have attended Syracuse. And if one of the state campuses in Florida uses its new tuition-setting freedom to create a measurable gap between its charges and those of other state campuses, it may lose some students.

It is clear, however, that for a significant proportion of college students, price is not the deciding factor. Students who do not apply for financial aid consistently report that academic reputation and other qualitative characteristics are the primary factors determining college choice. But the story is quite different for students with more limited financial resources. These students have much more elastic demand — they are much more concerned about changes in tuition levels and differentials across schools. Financial constraints are very real for students from low-income families and increasingly for those from middle-income families. Their college choice behavior reflects these constraints. This difference in price sensitivity among different subsets of students is an important explanation for the widespread practice of price discrimination within higher education.

Student Response to Tuition Levels

There is considerable evidence that for many students, price is a significant factor in the decision to enroll in college and in the choice of a college or university. Many schools are now offering financial aid packages designed to lower the net price to desirable students and are finding this strategy successful.

In 1995, Muskingum College in Ohio announced a $4,000 tuition cut and saw a significant increase in enrollments, at least in the short run. In other words, many colleges clearly face downward sloping demand curves and find students sensitive to the prices they charge.

However, the *elasticity of demand* for college varies considerably among different groups. Low-income students appear to have much more elastic demand than higher-income students. This is true both in terms of the decision to continue education after high school and in terms of choosing a particular institution. Students from families able and willing to pay $25,000 in college costs do not generally change their choice of school because of a $2,000 or $3,000 price differential. It is not surprising that the choices of lower-income students are more sensitive to price differences.

High-priced colleges do not just face relatively inelastic demand among students whose families can afford to pay. Some students may be even more eager to enroll when the sticker price is higher. Because of the difficulty of judging the quality of a college or university, signals of apparent quality are important in this market. While a beautiful campus with expensive facilities does not necessarily indicate high quality faculty, it creates the impression of a well-funded institution. A high tuition level may also be interpreted as a signal of high quality. It seems that there is something of a "Chivas Regal effect" in higher education. For institutions in the upper tier of the market, lowering their price might have the effect of indicating decreased quality—or decreased prestige—and might actually deter some students from enrolling. Higher tuition levels might actually increase demand among some groups of students.

Price Discrimination

Many products are sold under circumstances that require the seller to charge the same price to all consumers. The supermarket generally sells crackers to every customer at the same price. There are other products whose sellers can charge different prices to different groups of consumers, depending on the consumers' willingness to pay. Airlines charge business passengers more than vacation travelers. Business travelers have inelastic demand, and are not likely to cancel their trips because of fare increases. Demand for vacation travel is much more elastic. Airlines manage to charge different prices to these different groups by imposing restrictions on the lower fares that business travelers are frequently unable to meet.

Charging different prices to different consumers is called *price discrimination*. If producers can price discriminate, charging each consumer the maximum amount he or she is willing to pay, they can reap higher profits than if they charge everyone a price low enough to get the last consumer into the market.

An example of price discrimination in academia is journal prices that are much higher for libraries than for individual subscribers. This price discrimination works only as long as the consumers can be prevented from trading. If individual faculty members were to pass their personal subscriptions on to the library, the pricing system would fall apart. If the supermarket tried to charge chocolate addicts more for candy than they charge dieters, the dieters would soon start buying candy at low prices and selling it to the chocolate addicts.

Colleges and universities price discriminate when they offer financial aid. The net price is different for different students, despite the fact that they are purchasing the same commodity. Need-based aid allows students with limited financial resources, who could not attend if they were charged the full sticker price, to pay a lower price. Need-based aid price discriminates on the basis of ability to pay. Other forms of student aid may price discriminate on the basis of willingness to pay. Highly qualified students may be less willing to pay for a particular college because they have a choice among several selective institutions. Less qualified students will be more willing to pay—they will have less elastic demand—because they have fewer options.

Price discrimination: Charging different prices to different customers for the same good or service even though the cost of supplying those customers is the same.

Both private and public colleges and universities have increased their non-need-based price discrimination in recent years. Athletic scholarships have long been commonplace. Scholarships based on test scores or grades are increasingly common, but they are controversial because they may divert limited funds away from needy students, limiting their educational opportunities. Using academic qualifications to differentiate among students is not, however, viewed as fundamentally unethical. Other criteria that have been used or considered as the basis for price discrimination among students are considerably more problematic. The national debate about race-based scholarships may be the most visible. Colleges concerned with using financial aid strategically to enroll larger or more desirable classes could entertain the possibility of using grant aid to charge different net prices to men and women, to science majors and humanities majors, or to students who visit campus and those who play hard-to-get. This form of price discrimination would clearly raise questions very different from those involved in the differential pricing structure generated by need-based student aid.

Equity and Efficiency

Engaging in constructive policy analysis requires selecting a set of criteria by which to evaluate alternatives. It is relatively easy to arrive at a consensus that the best policies are those that are both efficient and fair, but arriving at a clear definition of these concepts is not so simple.

Although it is certainly reasonable to debate the importance of efficiency relative to other priorities, it is quite straightforward to define *efficiency* in terms of using resources as productively as possible. An economy or an enterprise that operates efficiently produces as much as possible, given the limited resources that are available. It is efficient to employ the most qualified workers available. It is inefficient to require attendance at lengthy meetings where nothing is accomplished. It is efficient to allocate grant dollars to students who will not enroll without financial aid instead of to students whose choices are not affected by the grant aid.

All of us have different views about what is fair and what is not. Ranking options in terms of equity almost always requires very subjective judgments. There are, however, two categories of equity frequently used by economists that can help to highlight significant characteristics of alternatives. *Horizontal equity* requires similar treatment of people in similar circumstances. All students who make the same mistakes on their exams should receive the same grade. Applicants in similar financial circumstances should be defined as having the same level of need that must be met in order for them to be able to afford to enroll. Faculty members in the same department, at the same rank and at the same level of seniority, who have similar levels of performance should be paid the same amount, whether they are male or female.

Vertical equity refers to the appropriately different ways in which people in different circumstances are treated. Like the federal income tax system, the financial aid need analysis system expects families with higher incomes to contribute a higher percentage of their incomes for their children's education. The logic is that the sacrifice required in giving up a certain fraction of income is greater for people with less discretionary income. Paying full professors more than associate professors in the same field who have been on the faculty for the same amount of time is vertically equitable. However, no simple rule of thumb is available to determine the amount by which these salaries should differ.

Efficiency and equity considerations are sometimes clearly compatible and at other times may appear to be conflicting. Cutting health care benefits to employees who have already retired might be efficient because it would save money without measurably changing anyone's behavior. But for equity reasons, few people would advocate such a move. It might seem fair to pay all new assistant professors the same salary but, in most situations, this would significantly hamper the institution's ability to attract qualified people for many positions. In this case, efficiency is likely to win out. In contrast, it seems both equitable and efficient to require all students to turn in their library books before they receive their diplomas. In any case, both equity and efficiency are important parts of the decision-making process.

Costs and Revenues: Total, Average, and Marginal

Profit-making firms are interested in maximizing the difference between their revenues and their costs. Despite their primary mission of providing educational opportunities, nonprofit colleges and universities must also pay considerable attention to managing both revenues and costs. Economists have some precise concepts that are useful in understanding many of the decisions colleges and universities face with respect not only to setting tuition and salaries and determining the optimal size of the student body, but also to developing and maintaining academic programs and supporting research.

The concept of *total cost is* simplest. It refers to all of the institution's expenditures over a certain period of time, such as an academic year. The economic concept of cost is different from the accounting concept in that it includes opportunity costs. A firm which is making a 1 percent rate of return on its investment will, for accounting purposes, have positive profits. But from an economic perspective, the opportunity cost of the invested funds — the return they could have generated in the best available alternative use — has to be taken into consideration. In economic terms, this firm is probably suffering losses, since its revenues do not cover its opportunity costs. Similarly, if a college enrolls 50 students to whom it grants tuition waivers, it does not actually give money to these students. But if these 50 students take the place of 50 paying students, then the tuition waivers constitute a very real cost.

Average cost is usually referred to as cost per student. If a university spends $100 million a year to educate 5,000 students, the average cost of education is $100 million divided by 5,000, or $20,000.

Does this mean that the college should not accept a student from whom it cannot collect $20,000 of tuition, unless it is making a conscious decision to take a loss on the student in order to provide equal opportunity or diversity in the student body or to in some other way purchase some benefit? No. The relevant concept for making this decision is *marginal cost*. Marginal cost is the change in total cost which results from producing one more unit — in this case from enrolling one additional student. As explained above in the discussion of the supply curve, for colleges and universities, the marginal cost of additional students is frequently very low — much lower than average cost. Once the classrooms and dormitories are built and the faculty hired, an extra student doesn't add much to the cost of operation. There is a limit to this of course. If the college decides to enroll two hundred additional students, it will probably have to hire additional personnel and expand facilities. But for most institutions, the marginal cost of a few extra students is quite low.

In order to determine whether the school's financial situation will improve with the enrollment of a student who pays say, $3,000 in tuition, the relevant question is whether or not $3,000 covers the marginal cost of educating the student. Does the student add more to revenues than she does to costs? If so, from a purely short-term financial perspective, the student should be enrolled. The same principle explains, for example, why airlines sell seats at low fares if they think they will not otherwise be filled. Once the plane is flying, the marginal cost of additional passengers is very low. Of course, if the total cost of flying an airliner with a capacity of 500 passengers is $350,000, the airline will lose money if it doesn't charge an average of at least $700 per person. But it makes sense to let an extra person come on board at the last minute even if he is willing to pay much less than this—just enough to cover food and any extra fuel cost resulting from the additional weight.

> **Marginal cost**: The amount by which producing an additional unit of a good or service increases total costs.
>
> **Marginal revenue**: The amount by which total revenue increases when an additional unit of a good or service is produced.
>
> **Marginal productivity**: The amount by which total output increases when an additional unit of a resource, such as labor, is employed.

Marginal Productivity

An efficient operation requires that resources be allocated to produce the greatest output for a given amount of input. In higher education, the difficulty involved in measuring output has caused us to place less emphasis on efficiency than is the case in other types of enterprises. But this difficulty should not prevent us from thinking carefully about how choices are made. An important economic principle is that resources allocated to different uses should generate the same benefit at the margin. In order to get the highest possible level of satisfaction from their limited budgets, consumers should make sure that the last dollar they spend on entertainment improves their well-being exactly as much as the last dollar they spend on clothing. If the last dollar spent on clothing buys more satisfaction, the consumer would be better off taking some money out of entertainment and buying more clothes. Similarly, in allocating one's time, it makes sense to spend a free hour in the most productive way possible. If the last hour spent on class preparation is more productive than the last hour spent on committee meetings, total productivity would be increased by canceling the meeting and preparing for class.

This marginal principle can be applied to expenditure decisions on campus. When deciding whether or not more money should be put into scientific equipment, some method should be devised to compare the benefit these extra dollars will generate in this use to the benefit they might generate if put into faculty salaries or student activity space. Of course, precise quantification of the benefits of many campus investments is impossible. Nonetheless, attempting to specify the positive impact of proposed undertakings and comparing the potential costs and benefits of alternatives is a prerequisite for efficient decision making. Most important is that the debate is not about whether scientific pursuits or rock concerts are more important. It is about the marginal benefit of putting the extra dollars into one endeavor or the other.

Economies of Scale and Scope

In some production processes, there may be *economies of scale*. The quantity of inputs does not have to double in order to double the quantity of outputs. Cost per unit may decline as the quantity produced increases because overhead costs can be spread over a larger number of units. Large supermarkets can sell their products at lower prices than those found at the corner store because of economies of scale. Some economies of scale certainly exist in higher education. A college with a hundred students would, for example, have difficulty supporting well-equipped physics laboratories or large athletic facilities.

Economies of scale occur when fixed costs are relatively high, but the variable costs of increasing levels of output are low. Building a college campus requires a very large outlay of resources. Once the college is built, the cost of the physical plant is fixed. It does not depend on how many students are educated on campus. But increased enrollments do require increases in other inputs — electricity, maintenance, staffing. The total cost of these inputs depends on the size of the student body. If the fixed costs are very large and adding additional students adds only small variable costs, there will be economies of scale.

In an economy dominated by giant multinational companies and in an environment where mergers between large companies are commonplace, it is easy to believe that economies of scale are pervasive. However, some production processes require fixed quantities of inputs to generate output. Technological advances have not reduced the amount of hairdresser time required to produce a stylish hair cut. Similarly, creating a superior seminar experience may require a ratio of no more than ten to fifteen students to one professor. Providing similar experiences for twice as many students would require twice as many faculty members.

Detecting where economies of scale exist is important. Colleges and universities may save considerable amounts of money by contracting out some activities to firms that specialize in say, food preparation, and can take advantage of economies of scale unattainable to campus-based operations. But it is equally important to recognize those activities where the search for economies of scale may reduce quality and even change the nature of the product, instead of increasing efficiency.

Economies of scope exist when firms can produce one product more efficiently because they also produce other related products. These advantages could result from the use of the same inputs or production facilities, from joint marketing programs, or from savings from a common management.

The Sony Corporation produces both sound equipment and televisions. They can produce these products more cheaply than two separate companies would be able to because of the overlapping technologies and because of the expertise one individual employee can contribute to both production processes. The company's reputation also facilitates the joint marketing of these products.

Most colleges and universities produce more than one output. Teaching and research are most common. The debate about whether research supports or detracts from the teaching mission of the institution is a well-known one. The argument that any resources devoted to research must be resources taken away from teaching is perhaps the simplest to understand. But the concept of economies of scope may be useful in seeing this issue differently. The knowledge and experience faculty members gain from their research can increase their effectiveness as teachers. The reputation an institution earns through the professional activities of its faculty may have a positive effect on the students who are attracted to campus, increasing the quality of education available. In other words, the two endeavors may complement each other quite effectively.

Market Structure: Competition Versus Monopoly Power

Market structure refers to the degree of competition that exists among firms in an industry. At one end of the continuum are *perfectly competitive* industries with many small firms, none of which have a big enough share of the market to noticeably influence price. At the other end of the continuum are monopolies, markets in which one firm operates without competition because no close substitutes are available. *Monopolies* can charge higher prices than other types of firms because they face no effective competition.

Firms in perfectly competitive industries sell products that are not readily distinguishable from the products of their competitors. Because it is virtually impossible for them to differentiate their products from those of others, they cannot raise their prices above the going price without losing their customers. If existing firms in a perfectly competitive industry are making high profits, others will choose to enter the industry, which by definition is characterized by easy entry and exit. This means that high profits will not persist. New firms entering will try to break into the market by charging a slightly lower price. This process will continue until the product price just covers average costs of production, and profit rates are comparable to those available elsewhere in the economy.

The market for eggs (in the absence of any government interference with prices) would be an example of perfect competition. The members of the egg industry have, at times, gotten together to advertise the "incredible edible egg" or to counter fears about eggs causing heart disease, because individual egg producers cannot succeed in making consumers think their eggs are any better than any other farmer's eggs. Prices of eggs tend to be fairly similar, since people are unlikely to pay significantly more for one brand than for another.

Higher education is clearly not a perfectly competitive industry. In the United States, we pride ourselves on the variety of postsecondary experiences available to students. There are two- and four-year colleges, large public research universities, and small colleges devoted solely to teaching. Students can choose residential campuses or distance learning, vocational programs or liberal arts education, urban settings or rural, ivy-covered walls. Schools with national name recognition can charge higher tuition than less well-known institutions without losing all of their applicants. More than half the students attending four-year institutions pay less than $4,000 in tuition and fees and almost three quarters pay less than $8,000 per year for their college educations,[5] while thousands choose private colleges and universities with price tags exceeding $30,000 per year. Price is clearly not the only — or even the primary — distinguishing factor.

While firms in perfectly competitive industries compete for customers on the basis of price, those in imperfectly competitive industries engage in non-price competition. Like perfect competition, *monopolistic competition* involves many small firms with minimal market power. But in this sort of industry, firms are able to differentiate their products, either through brand identification or through slight differences in the characteristics of their products. Firms in monopolistic competition will be able to charge higher prices if they can create brand loyalty, but because there are close substitutes produced by competing firms, they, like firms in perfect competition, are not likely to maintain high profits over the long run. The clothing industry is monopolistically competitive. People are willing to pay higher prices for brand names, but there are many firms in the industry and new firms can easily enter to compete with existing firms.

Because of the large number of colleges and universities in this country, it is reasonable to choose the model of monopolistic competition as most appropriate to describe this industry. One college's education can be substituted for another despite the considerable amount of differentiation that exists. For most institutions, the demand curve is quite elastic because there are other schools in the market that are close substitutes. There is considerable non-price competition, but if an individual school raises its price significantly above the prices of competing schools, it will lose enrollments. This phenomenon causes the prices of the competing schools to be within a narrow range of each other.

It may, however, be more useful to think of higher education as consisting of several smaller markets, each including a group of schools that compete intensely with each other for students and that are aware of each other's circumstances and strategies. Colleges frequently have lists of the schools with which they compare themselves — schools with overlapping applications and acceptances. These peer groups of schools tend to compete intensely with each other using characteristics other than price. If one highly selective New England liberal arts college builds fancy new athletic facilities, others are likely to follow suit. If one Catholic college in the Midwest institutes an honors program, other similar schools in their market may feel compelled to do the same. It could be argued that in the state of Utah, where there are nine colleges and universities and about 80 percent of students attend in-state institutions, there is an effective oligopoly.

In an *oligopoly*, a small number of firms dominate the market. In the for-profit sector, these firms are likely to earn profit levels higher than those enjoyed by firms in more competitive industries. Some industries are dominated by a small number of firms because barriers to entry make it difficult for new firms to enter and compete with existing firms. Entering the automobile industry is a challenge both because of the large amount of capital that is required to produce cars and because of the extent to which consumers depend on brand names to trust the safety of the cars

5. The College Board, *Trends in College Pricing*, 2000, p. 3.

they purchase. Coca-Cola and Pepsi Cola maintain their hold on the soft drink market simply because their successful advertising has created such intense brand loyalty that consumers are not particularly interested in cheaper substitutes. The medical industry limits the numbers of doctors by restricting access to medical education and becoming a taxi driver in New York City is difficult because of the small number of medallions available. Economies of scale — average costs that decline as the level of output increases — explain why new entrants are rare in utilities.

Schools that effectively compete with only a few other schools are operating in oligopolistic markets. For example, the Ivy League is an oligopoly. In an oligopoly, each firm is watching other firms carefully and is engaging in strategic behavior. The recent changes in financial aid policies among the Ivy Leagues schools are a good example of oligopolistic patterns. If one school raises its price significantly, it can lose students to other schools. But if it lowers its price, the other schools are likely to follow suit and no one will benefit. So in these markets, as in competitive markets, prices are likely to be clustered together.

The fact that new private colleges and universities are relatively rare is also a sign of barriers to entry. The number of public institutions, particularly community colleges, grew rapidly in the 1970s. But the only new private institutions have been in the for-profit sector. Enterprises like the University of Phoenix are in fact developing a market that, while a close substitute for traditional colleges and universities, is quite separate. It caters to a different population and offers a very different service.

What are the barriers to entry for traditional colleges and universities? Clearly, reputation is one. Because of the imperfect information available to students, trusting that their college will provide a quality education is critical. Moreover, students expect a significant return on their education when they enter the labor market. Because it is difficult for potential employers to measure the productivity of job applicants, the reputations of the institutions whose degrees the applicants hold become important signals in the labor market, making it more difficult for new colleges to gain a foothold.

Another barrier to entry is created by the wealth that has been accumulated by many successful private colleges. Without endowment or access to donations from alumni, new institutions would have considerable difficulty competing in the traditional nonprofit higher education market.

These barriers to entry mean that while there is a large number of colleges and universities and considerable competition among them for students, many institutions do have considerable protection from market forces. Some critics would argue that this protection has allowed colleges and universities to operate inefficiently for too long. Others would argue that these barriers to entry provide an important cushion for institutions struggling to maintain their focus on access to quality educational opportunities, rather than on the bottom line.

Few industries fit exactly into any one of the market structures described above. Still, the models highlight the relevance of competition and of monopoly power in understanding pricing and production policies. The model of monopolistic competition is very useful in understanding the national market for higher education. On many campuses, considerable effort is put into trying to make the institution appear unique so students will consider other schools poor substitutes. Still, students have many options in postsecondary education.

The oligopoly model provides different insights. Many institutional policy makers are keenly aware of the policies and innovations of their competitors and actively engage in strategic behavior; they are not threatened by the significantly lower prices in different segments of the market.

The College Antitrust Case

In the early 1990s, the Justice Department pursued an antitrust case against a large group of private colleges. The government contended that the colleges were violating antitrust laws in setting financial aid, tuition, and faculty salary levels.

A major focus of the case was the Overlap Group—a group of 23 colleges that met every year to discuss financial aid awards to students accepted at more than one college in the group. The colleges, the most selective in the country, held these discussions in order to diminish price competition. They wanted students to choose schools based on factors other than price and designed aid packages to make the price of one school to an individual student the same as the price of any other school in the Overlap Group. They agreed to meet the financial needs of accepted candidates in full and to distribute aid only on the basis of measured financial need.

The Justice Department argued that this practice constituted collusion and price fixing, and violated anti-trust laws. All of the colleges involved except MIT signed a consent decree, agreeing to end this practice. MIT went to court, arguing that the law should treat the colleges as charitable organizations rather than as businesses. They are nonprofit entities whose purpose is to provide education and they subsidize all of their students. The case was settled in 1993 and colleges now have carefully defined ways in which they are allowed to share financial aid information.

Sticker prices at selective private colleges are still very close to each other, but since the Justice Department intervened, there has been much more competition among schools in financial aid policies. Non-need based, strategic use of financial aid is widespread. The most selective colleges still base their aid awards on need, but they publicly modify their criteria for determining need in ways clearly designed to attract students.

The level of cooperation that did—and still does—occur among colleges and universities is a clear sign of oligopoly. The schools know who their competitors are and they act strategically in setting their prices. The motivation is very different from the motivation behind the practices the antitrust laws were designed to prevent. But the economic model can help us to understand and predict how colleges make their decisions.

Concepts in College Finance

C ollege finance differs in a variety of ways from both personal finance and for-profit business finance. For this reason, many faculty and staff are unfamiliar with the concepts and principles underlying campus financial deliberations. Clarifying the terminology and the building blocks of college financing should help all constituencies to be more valuable participants in campus discussions and debates. The American Association of University Professors articulated this need when they said of faculty involvement in budgetary decisions, "Involvement alone will not do the job; only informed involvement will protect our academic programs and concerns."[1] More information about the fundamental financial realities of the institution should create an atmosphere more conducive to respectful dialogue and compromise.

Revenues

One of the hurdles to engaging the college community in a reasoned discussion of the intersection of finances and institutional mission is that it is easier to focus on the expenditures educational institutions make in the process of accomplishing their goals than on the revenues required to support these expenditures or on the difficulty of balancing the two. When we think of profit-making businesses, we think of their essence as making money—generating revenues. Clothing stores and automobile makers and banks provide useful goods and services. But they provide these services because they can make a profit by doing so, not because their primary focus is the well-being or improved living standards of their customers.

Colleges and universities, on the other hand, exist because of the service they provide—not because of the money they can make providing that service. Most college faculty and administrators could have pursued more lucrative careers, but they have chosen not to put money at the top of their priority list. Moreover, their function at work is not to maximize the institution's revenues. Of course, those responsible for an institution's finances have a different focus from those hired to teach sociology, but everyone agrees that the purpose of financial strength is to be able to provide quality educational opportunities—not the other way around.

This reality makes it difficult for many—particularly faculty—to discuss comfortably ways that an institution might enhance its revenues. Focusing on generating

---

1. *Academe*, November/December 1989, p. 9.

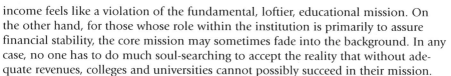

income feels like a violation of the fundamental, loftier, educational mission. On the other hand, for those whose role within the institution is primarily to assure financial stability, the core mission may sometimes fade into the background. In any case, no one has to do much soul-searching to accept the reality that without adequate revenues, colleges and universities cannot possibly succeed in their mission.

Revenues come from a variety of sources, and those sources differ significantly depending on whether the institution is in the public sector or the private sector. As indicated in Table 3, public institutions are dependent on state legislatures for about 36 percent of their revenues, whereas at private institutions, federal and state monies combined constitute only about 16 percent of total revenues. Tuition and fees, on the other hand, are close to half of private higher education revenues, but about one-fifth of revenues in the public sector.[2]

Not revealed in the table is the considerable variation in revenue sources within the public and private sectors. For example, public research universities that receive large amounts of federal support get only 15 percent of their revenues from student tuition and fees, compared to 31 percent for public undergraduate colleges.. The same categories in the private sector get 23 percent and 59 percent of their revenues, respectively, from tuition and fees. At theological schools and private colleges specializing in religion, endowment income provides 14 percent of revenues, compared to 6 percent at major research universities.[3]

Among private institutions, there is also a wide range in the degree of dependency on private donations. Many schools receive annual gifts from alumni and friends. More fortunate institutions have enough well-heeled friends to have accumulated significant endowments. This form of accumulated wealth generates income that can supplement tuition and fees in the operating budget. For a few schools, this income is very large. Harvard University's endowment of close to $20 billion is the largest in the country, with Yale University and the University of Texas, each with about half that amount, a distant second and third. As of June 30, 1999, 34 institutions had endowments exceeding $1 billion. These included seven public institutions or

Table 3. Current Fund Revenue of Four-Year Institutions of Higher Education.

	Public	Private
Tuition and fees	19%	43%
Federal government	11%	14%
State governments	36%	2%
Local governments	4%	1%
Private gifts, grants, contracts	4%	9%
Endowment income	1%	5%
Sales and services	22%	21%
Other	3%	5%

Source: Digest of Education Statistics, 1999, Tables 332 and 333.

2. Digest of Education Statistics, 1999, Table 332.
3. National Center for Education Statistics, Digest of Education Statistics, 1999, Table 336.

systems. Of the approximately 3,900 degree-granting higher education institutions, 2,200 are private nonprofit. About 20 percent have endowments exceeding $150 million and fewer than 500 have endowments exceeding $6 million.[4]

Endowment

> **Endowment:** Assets held by the institution that must be invested to generate income. Endowment funds are donated with the restriction that the principal cannot be used at all. In order for the purchasing power of the endowment to be maintained, the assets must be allowed to grow at least at the rate of inflation.
>
> **Quasi-endowment:** Funds set aside by the institution to be invested to generate income. However, these funds can be used at the discretion of the institution.

An endowment is essentially the institution's monetary wealth. The institution has other wealth in the form of land, buildings, and equipment. The endowment consists of funds that have been donated to the institution, either with a specific purpose attached to them (restricted funds) or for whatever purpose the college deems appropriate. Unlike annual giving funds, which are generally spent during the year they are received, endowment gifts cannot be spent. They must be invested and only the income — or a fraction of the income — they generate can be spent through the operating budget. The college has no choice about this. This is a condition frequently attached to gifts. But even if there were a choice, it would be short-sighted of the institution not to choose to build an endowment.

> **Unrestricted funds:** Assets that can be used for any purpose at the discretion of the institution.
>
> **Restricted funds:** Funds that may be used only according to the restrictions imposed by a contractual agreement such as that specified by a donor wishing to fund a particular activity.

Each institution adopts a spending rule that allows a certain percentage of its endowment to go into the operating budget each year. This percentage is the take-out rate. For most institutions, this rate is about 5 percent. If all of the endowment earnings were spent, the value of the endowment would decline in real terms because of inflation. The endowment should at least retain its purchasing power from year to year, even without new contributions. But there is not one right answer to what the take-out rate should be. This is a decision for which the financial administrators of the college should be expected to have a thoughtful explanation.

Endowment wealth and spending rules can be a source of tension on campus. Some faculty may resent the idea that the institution is accumulating endowment wealth at the same time that salaries are growing at what seem to be unacceptably slow rates or restrictions are being placed on program innovations. It is quite

---

4. *The Chronicle of Higher Education*, February 18, 2000; Kit Lively and Scott Street, "The Rich Get Richer," *The Chronicle of Higher Education*, October 13, 2000.

possible to focus on the accumulation of financial wealth to the extent that the current goals of the educational institution are insufficiently supported, and this possibility should always be kept in mind. But it is the endowment that provides long-term security for the institution and ensures the successful perpetuation of the college's mission. Just as families without savings risk financial crises when unexpected emergencies arise, institutions without endowment income may be unable to withstand periods of declining enrollment, unexpected inflation in the prices of energy or other inputs, or a weak economy that diminishes family ability to pay. The endowment might be viewed as a form of self-insurance. Certainly any organization that has lifetime employment contracts with a significant fraction of its employees is well advised to have a significant store of liquid wealth. In periods of unusual financial stress, it may be possible to increase the take-out rate without violating the endowment principal. Ongoing discussions of the appropriate balance between current needs and future protection will never lead to a consensus, but it should dispel misunderstanding and relieve some of the tension over this issue.

The tenuous relationship between the apparent wealth of the institution and the funds available for current spending may be particularly frustrating to faculty during and immediately following capital campaigns. The university is proudly announcing that it has received millions of dollars in gifts and at the same time is pressing for cost-saving measures on campus. A successful campaign certainly strengthens an institution's financial position. Faculty members are correct to expect to see the effects of this strength reflected in compensation, in curricular opportunities, or in research support. But the magnitude of the new opportunities is likely to be much smaller than many would anticipate. First, much of the money pledged in the campaign will not actually be in the college's hands for years to come. Some donations are made gradually over time. Others will not be available to the institution until the death of the donor. Moreover, once the institution does have the money in hand, it frequently must be added to the endowment, and only about 5 percent of it will be available for increased annual expenditures. In addition, the gross amount of money raised must be adjusted for the amount it cost the college to mount the campaign. So millions of dollars can quickly become hundreds of thousands of dollars in the annual institutional budget.

Tax Revenues

For public institutions, it is tax revenues, not endowments and private giving, that provide the main supplement to tuition revenues. As recently as 1980-81, tuition and fees provided only about 13 percent of public college and university revenues, with state government contributing nearly half, and the federal government providing about as much as tuition revenues. But over the last two decades, state funding has declined to just over a third of total revenues, while tuition and fees now constitute about 19 percent.[5] The increasing role of tuition in the funding of public sector higher education makes discussion of tuition central on all college and university campuses.

---

5. National Center for Education Statistics, *Digest of Education Statistics, 1999*, Table 336.

Tuition Revenues: Gross Versus Net

One significant ambiguity involved in measuring institutional revenues has to do with the distinction between gross tuition revenues and net tuition revenues. Gross tuition revenue is calculated by multiplying the number of matriculating students by the tuition charge. This is the standard way of thinking about this budget item. However, many students do not pay the full stated tuition—the sticker price. Rather the college gives them a scholarship or financial aid. Essentially, they are receiving a price discount.

Suppose the sticker price is $18,000. A student is awarded an institutional grant of $5,000 because of her family's financial circumstances. In this case, the institution actually collects $13,000 of revenue. This is the price being charged to this particular student. Counting the entire $18,000 as revenue and $5,000 as an expenditure is basically the same as a car dealer's counting the sticker price of $25,000 as revenue, and considering your $3,000 discount an expenditure when you have bargained him down and ended up paying only $22,000 for your car.

Net tuition revenue refers to the amount of tuition revenue the college actually receives. It is the sum of the actual prices paid by each student. It can also be calculated by subtracting institutional grant awards from gross tuition revenue. The bottom line is the same, but the implications are different. If gross revenue is the focus, there is a sense that the $5,000 spent could have been devoted to financial aid or to computers or to faculty salaries. There is a decision to be made about expenditure priorities. On the other hand, if net revenues are the focus, the choices are more limited. The $13,000 student would probably not have enrolled if the price were $18,000, so deciding how to spend the extra $5,000 is unrealistic. For a small number of institutions, it would probably be possible to attract a full class of students willing to pay the sticker price with no discounts. But for most colleges and universities, net revenue is a more reasonable starting point for discussions of expenditure priorities.

Expenditures

On the expenditure side, the instruction category is only a part of the activity the college or university must fund. Research, student services, and operation and maintenance of plant are among the other necessary expenditure categories. The breakdown of expenditures by category clearly points to important questions worthy of an ongoing discussion. Has the proportion of total expenditures devoted to instruction declined over time? If so, why? A clear understanding of this information can facilitate a more constructive dialogue about institutional priorities.

Budget Categories

The operating budget provides a good starting point for understanding how colleges and universities spend their money.

> **Instruction:** This most basic category theoretically includes all expenses for instruction, including research that is not separately budgeted. This is where faculty salaries appear.

Academic support: This category includes support services that are an integral part of the primary mission of instruction, research, and public service; it includes libraries, museums, computing support, academic administration, curriculum development, etc.

Student services: Expenditures for recruitment and admission. Registrar, student life, co-curricular, and residential life expenses fall into this category.

Institutional support: This covers day-to-day operational support except for the physical plant. It includes general administrative services, legal and fiscal operations, personnel and records, and campus security.

Operation and maintenance of plant: Utilities, custodial service, property insurance, repairs, renovations, etc. are accounted for here.

Mandatory transfers: Funds that must be transferred to meet legal obligations. These include debt service on campus buildings.

Other: Institutional budgets also include separate categories for scholarships and fellowships, for research, and for public service.

Each institution sets its own expenditure priorities, and the processes through which these priorities are determined vary across campuses. Nonetheless, both the shared economic and demographic environment and competition within the higher education industry contribute to patterns in institutional pricing and expenditure decisions. It is not unusual, for example, for many colleges with overlapping applicants to enhance their sports facilities at about the same time. In recent years, declining state support has led to tuition increases in many public higher education systems. In the private sector, the failure of publicly funded aid to keep up with increasing costs of attendance and decreasing family ability to pay has led to a general increase in the weight of student aid in institutional budgets. In both sectors, fiscal constraints and uncertainty have led to increased reliance on part-time and other nontenure-track faculty positions. Chapter 4 on campus issues discusses this trend in greater detail.

These trends contribute to the fact that instruction is a smaller component of education and general expenses on both public and private campuses than it was 20 years ago. (These are current fund expenditures, excluding hospitals, dining halls, and other auxiliary enterprises.) Between 1980-81 and 1995-96, the portion of education and general expenditures devoted to instruction fell in the public sector, from 43 percent to 40 percent. This decline and a proportionately much larger decline in expenditures on plant and facilities maintenance have been balanced by small increases in most other areas. The largest increases were in research, which went from 11 to 13 percent of the budget, and scholarships and fellowships, which increased from 3 to 5 percent.[6]

Similarly, in the private sector, instruction has fallen from 37 to 35 percent of expenditures. Student services have, as the common wisdom would predict,

6. Ibid., Table 346.

increased—from 6 to 7 percent of education and general expenditures. But the most dramatic shift has been in scholarships and fellowships. Fifteen percent of private college and university budgets is now devoted to institutional grant aid, compared to 9 percent two decades ago. In addition to the decline in the share of expenditures devoted to instruction, research has declined from 12 to 10 percent and maintenance of plant and equipment from 11 to 8 percent of education and general expenses.[7]

The across-the-board decline in expenditures for the operation and maintenance of plant may represent a decision to concentrate funds in the areas where they will have the most direct effect on the quality of education the institution is providing. Alternatively, this change could reflect difficulty in making money-saving decisions with immediately visible costs and a tendency to defer the pain—in the form of deferred maintenance—as a way of settling differences among constituencies on campus.

Salaries Versus Compensation

Annual debates on campus about salary increases could be enhanced by a clearer distinction between salaries and total compensation. Compensation includes both salary—current cash income—and benefits. Some of the benefits received by faculty and staff are in the form of cash and others are *in-kind* benefits. Contributions to retirement funds are cash paid out now by the institution, but received in the future by the employees. Health insurance is an in-kind benefit that will be used to different extents by different employees. Some benefits are discretionary and can be negotiated. The institution may alter the amount it contributes to pension funds, the percentage of health care premiums covered, or the amount of life insurance it provides. On the other hand, it has no choice about the contributions it makes to the Social Security and unemployment compensation funds in the names of employees.

It is easy for employees to think only in terms of salary, since it is the size of their paychecks that has the most immediate effect on their daily lives. On the other hand, it is too easy for financial officers to focus exclusively on total compensation, since salary and benefits affect the budget similarly. Clearly, increases in the cost of health coverage for employees must be offset either by decreases in other expenditures or by increases in revenue. On the other hand, employees are not better off because their health insurance has gotten more expensive, and this type of compensation increase is unlikely to satisfy employees struggling to make ends meet.

Financial Aid

Expenditures on financial aid deserve special attention because they are claiming larger and larger portions of the budget. This is particularly true in the private sector, but is also occurring to a considerable degree in the public sector. Moreover, as discussed above, it is not clear that expenditures on financial aid can always be traded off for expenditures on other priorities. The use of financial aid funds to fill classes and attract particular types of students is increasingly central to the plans of many

---

7. Ibid., Table 347.

institutions and anyone who expects to be fully engaged in campus decision-making processes will be well served by familiarity with the basic components of the student aid system.

Early federal scholarship programs were motivated by a national desire to train more scientists and assure the United States' position in international competition. But the foundation of the existing large and complex student aid system is the American dream of equal opportunity. In the early 1970s, with the War on Poverty in full swing, the federal government introduced the Pell Grant Program (known then as Basic Educational Opportunity Grants, or BEOG). The idea was that insufficient financial resources should not be a barrier to access to higher education for any American.

Over the last 30 years, the student aid system has grown dramatically and has evolved in some unexpected and unplanned ways. While federal grant aid remains an important cornerstone of the system, the federal loan system has grown to dominate it. Originally a program where the federal government guaranteed loans made by banks to students, this program now also involves loans made directly from the federal government to students. In addition, the loan program that subsidizes loans for students with documented financial need by paying the interest while they are in college is now supplemented by an unsubsidized loan program available to all students, as well as a parent loan program that grants creditworthy parents of undergraduate students access to all the funds required to cover the cost of education. More recently, the federal government has added a system of tuition tax credits to the grant and loan programs.

Because of the elaborate federal programs, as well as the existence of state-funded aid programs, even colleges and universities that do not have significant funds of their own to distribute have active financial aid offices. But as the trends in expenditure patterns indicate, growing amounts of institutional dollars are being funneled into student aid. At schools where the dollar amount directed toward this function is sizable, financial aid is, and will continue to be, at the core of many campus discussions about spending priorities.

As explained in Chapter 2, when a college uses grant aid to effectively charge different prices to different students, it is engaged in the process of price discrimination. Some students are paying the full sticker price to attend the institution. They receive a bill for the full, published charge for tuition and fees and, if applicable, for room and board. They send a check and the college adds the amount to its revenues. This is money that the institution can spend as it sees fit.

Other students get bills for smaller amounts. While the full sticker price is quoted to them, they are told that their account has already been credited with a scholarship or grant amount. They write a smaller check and the college's bank account, the amount available for discretionary spending, grows by a smaller amount.

The college has granted a price discount to those students who have received grants or scholarships. The college calculates its discount rate as the percentage of gross revenue it forgoes through the awarding of institutional aid. According to data collected by the National Association of College and University Business Officers, on average, private colleges are discounting by close to 40 percent.[8] In other words, the

---

8. Bureau of the Census, op.cit., Table 694.

tuition revenue collected is about 40 percent less than what it would be if all students paid the full sticker price and about 40 percent less than it appears to be if financial aid is viewed as an expenditure and gross revenues are reported. This phenomenon is extremely important to discussions both of college affordability and of institutional financing options.

If, in discussions about campus priorities, the decision emerges that fewer dollars should be devoted to student aid, the simplest approach would be to look at the operating budget, assume total revenues are constant, and decrease the amount under student aid, adding those dollars saved into the columns for computers or faculty salaries. That is, the easiest way to think about this is to treat financial aid like any other expenditure that can be modified according to current institutional priorities.

But at many institutions a serious problem will arise with this procedure. If less money is devoted to financial aid, some students who would otherwise have enrolled may choose to attend other schools. They may go to schools that give them more generous aid awards, to schools with lower sticker prices, or to schools that offer more of the attributes they are seeking, despite comparable prices. In other words, an institution that cuts its aid budget may find that it enrolls a smaller class and that its revenues do not meet expectations.

The importance of this phenomenon differs from campus to campus, but it is one of which anyone engaged in budget debates must be aware. The implication is not that every dollar of financial aid is well spent or is a dollar that brings in more revenue. Rather, the implication is that the effects of financial aid expenditures should be studied carefully on every campus. The first question relates to the purpose of financial aid. Every campus aid office was set up to administer federal funds, which are based on student and family ability to pay and, where money is available, to allocate institutional funds in order to provide access to education for students with limited financial resources. But financial aid now serves multiple purposes on many campuses.

How each institution can and should face the dilemmas presented by student aid depends on individual circumstances as well as underlying philosophy. This is one of the campus issues discussed in the following chapter.

Economic Realities

Inflation

Like any financial entity, colleges and universities have to plan for and respond to external economic realities. Everyone on campus is aware of the fact that unexpected inflation can disrupt the best-laid plans. Inflation is a general increase in the prices of goods and services. If the rate of inflation increases, it means that prices are rising more rapidly than they were previously. When inflation is anticipated, an institution can plan for it. If everyone expects prices to rise by 5 percent next year, they can budget accordingly. Both employers and employees will know that a 5 percent wage increase will keep workers' purchasing power constant. Unanticipated inflation causes more problems. The amounts allocated in budgets turn out to be insufficient to cover expenses. People who have loaned money find themselves being paid back in dollars worth less than they had expected. Employees find that they can't buy as many goods and services with their paychecks as they could in the past. Students and families feel less able to pay for college.

There are several ways to measure the rate of inflation. The most common measure is the Consumer Price Index (CPI). This index, compiled by the Department of Commerce, measures the change in the price of a market basket of goods typically purchased by consumers. If wage increases are exactly equal to increases in the CPI, workers find that they are able to buy the same goods and services each year. Only if wage increases exceed the CPI will workers find that they have more purchasing power—that is, higher real wages.

Many colleges and universities refer not only to the CPI, but also to the Higher Education Price Index (HEPI). Designed by Research Associates of Washington[9] to measure changes in the prices of the goods and services colleges and universities purchase for their current operation, the HEPI is sometimes used to explain or to argue for increased funding levels. The HEPI tends to rise more rapidly than the CPI, in part because faculty and staff salaries should evidence some increased purchasing power over time. For example, during the decade from 1987 to 1997, the CPI rose 41 percent, while the HEPI increased by 48 percent.[10] This index also tends to fluctuate less than the CPI, since the HEPI is driven primarily by compensation levels. It is important to understand that while the HEPI is a good indicator of the growth in revenues needed to sustain institutional budgets, it is not a reasonable indicator of how rapidly salaries should grow. This is the case both because salary increases are among the main factors causing HEPI to increase and because the goods and services on which HEPI is based are not those purchased by the employees.

Faculty/Staff Salaries and the CPI

It is quite common for college and university employees—like other workers—to seek salary increases commensurate with the rate of growth of consumer prices. This is quite reasonable, since no one wants to lose purchasing power and experience a decline in standard of living. But the solution may not be perfect.

If average salaries on campus rise with the CPI, the real standard of living will remain constant. Although real wages in the United States were declining or stagnant in the 1980s and early 1990s, we would be quite distressed if we were able to buy only the same goods and services that were within the reach of our grandparents. The real goal on campus is for salaries to rise more rapidly than the CPI.

Individual salaries do not necessarily move together with average salaries. Individuals frequently expect their earnings to rise more rapidly than the average salary as they move up the ladder of seniority. As older workers retire and new workers are hired, continuing employees can see their wages rise more rapidly than the CPI, without that being the case for the average salary. Confusion may also arise over the difference between changes in the compensation budget and in the typical

9. Research Associates of Washington, 2605 Klingle Road, N.W., Washington, D.C. 20008.
10. U.S. Department of Commerce, *Statistical Abstract of the United States, 1999*, Table 314.

salary. An increase in the compensation pool could be driven either by more dollars being directed towards continuing employees or by an increase in the total number of employees.

If the compensation pool rises with the CPI, revenues must also rise that rapidly. Personnel costs constitute considerably more than half of campus expenditures. If other expenditures — on technology, energy or financial aid, for example—rise more rapidly than the CPI, salaries can be maintained in real terms only if revenues rise more rapidly than the CPI. Public complaints about the cost of attending college rising more rapidly than the general price level are grounded in a very real phenomenon. Faculty salaries generally rose more rapidly than the CPI in the 1980s and 1990s, but are just now reaching the level required to compensate for the significant decline in their purchasing power that occurred during the 1970s.

Productivity

In the economy at large, productivity increases facilitate increased purchasing power for workers. Productivity, or output per worker, tends to increase over time because of technological progress. This increase in productivity allows wages to increase without putting upward pressure on product prices.

Productivity is measured most easily in industries where the output can be quantified without difficulty. Between 1988 and 1997, output per hour rose at an annual rate of about 7 percent in communications equipment, 3 percent in the beverage industry, and 1 percent in paper mills. Over the same period, productivity fell in cable television and eating and drinking establishments.[11]

Defining and measuring productivity in higher education is not so simple. The number of students receiving course credit or degrees can be counted, but few people would argue that these numbers alone are a reasonable measure of institutional output. The quality of educational services and the specific benefits accruing to individual students are the core of the institutional mission but are impossible to quantify or even describe precisely. Nonetheless, the goals of higher education certainly constitute a form of output, and it is clear that, as in many other service industries, productivity increases are harder to come by than in manufacturing. In order to allow compensation to increase without putting upward pressure on tuition, faculty would have to teach more students. Since this could reduce the quality of the education being produced, it may not be a good way to measure progress. This means that the price of education is likely to rise more rapidly than the prices of many other products — and more rapidly than the CPI. Similar problems occur in other industries that require that service providers be physically present with clients or customers, with the personal relationship placing limits on the scale at which the service can be performed and on the possibilities for cutting costs. The tension between salary increases that allow faculty and staff to maintain their relative position in society and rapidly rising tuition levels has been and will continue to be a problem for policymakers in higher education.

---

11. Bureau of the Census, op.cit., Table 694.

Campus Issues

T his chapter examines four issues that may cause tensions on many campuses. First is the question of the extent to which it is reasonable or useful to view a college or university as a business. Will this perspective increase efficiency and perhaps free resources that might enhance the educational mission? Will it undermine the core institutional values? The second and third sections deal with two sensitive personnel issues: compensation and tenure. The discussions here are not intended to bolster any particular position on these major issues but to present information and analytical perspectives that might mitigate the emotional nature of typical debates on these subjects. The fourth section addresses the question of financial aid and the competing targets of merit and need. The approaches used in the discussion of these four issues should be applicable to a variety of other problems on many campuses.

Should We Think of a College as a Business?

Faculty members often have strong negative reactions to the idea of applying concepts and principles from the for-profit business world to the management of higher education institutions. Using the language of business firms—customers, demand, product—is frequently viewed as denigrating the educational and intellectual mission. Colleges and universities have missions very different from those of firms producing goods and services for profit. When board members with fiduciary responsibilities look to the business sector for models of organization and management, the potential for serious clashes with campus values and culture is great. Nonetheless, the lessons of recent years have shown that it is impossible to protect the academy entirely from market forces and like any other enterprise, higher education institutions face very real resource constraints. Perhaps demystifying some of the market terminology while taking a close look at ways in which colleges differ from other enterprises can facilitate a dialogue on the subject.

Students as Customers

Perhaps most grating to the academic ear is the use of the word *customers* to represent students. The simple transaction of a customer exchanging money for a clearly defined good or service is a poor representation of the relationship between a

student and her college. The college provides an environment in which a student can work to become educated. The fact that students are paying faculty to teach them is generally far below the surface in their interactions. Rather, they are engaged in a cooperative enterprise with a shared goal.

Nonetheless, college students are customers, although they are very different from most customers. One significant difference is that students cannot benefit from the education they are purchasing unless they bring considerable effort and ability to the task. Moreover, students constitute a major input into the process of producing education since the quality of a student's education is dramatically affected by the other students on campus. The quality of your television, in contrast, is unaffected by the character of the other people who buy similar televisions.

No matter what the efforts of faculty and staff, no matter how extensive the facilities, no college or university can produce quality education without quality students. For this reason, colleges and universities are not generally willing to sell their product to everyone who is willing to pay. If they did this, they would end up with a deteriorating product. There are few firms in other industries that turn away customers who are willing to pay because they don't meet the *admission standards*. But if colleges having trouble filling their classes forget about the impact the composition of the student body has on the quality of their product, they are in danger of losing their ability to deliver quality education. This means that colleges must market themselves to desirable students not only to gain tuition revenues, but also to assure that they maintain the ability to provide high-quality education.

Most prospective students — or potential customers — are not in a position to make the kind of informed choices they make in other markets. Informed consumers are a necessary part of the competitive economy that is supposed to create efficient outcomes. If consumer information is imperfect, markets will not operate efficiently because consumers will not always gravitate to the lowest-cost producer for equivalent products, nor will they be able to accurately weigh the costs and benefits of their purchases.

Standard examples of market failure involving incomplete information include markets for medical care, where consumers must rely on suppliers for information about the need for services and the quality of those services. In the case of higher education, there are several related problems. The consumers are often young people. They have no experience with higher education and may underestimate its value. Their desire for immediate gratification and undervaluing of future benefits may cause young people to choose the job market (or a life of leisure) over investing in themselves through education, even if this choice is inefficient in the long run.

Consumers of education cannot research college choices as efficiently as they do the purchase of an automobile, partly because of the difficulty of measuring outcomes. They are unlikely to know exactly what outcome they want and they are not able to entirely appreciate the offerings until after they have already benefited from them. Even after students have completed their schooling, it is not a simple task to compare the value of one institution to another, or even the value of a college education to years spent in the labor force. The nonmonetary benefits are almost impossible to fully define, much less measure. But even the value of the short-term financial benefit of a specific educational experience for a particular individual is elusive, given the impossibility of controlled experiments and of sampling alternative choices. A full understanding of what education can do for one's life (other than increasing earnings) will develop over the lifetime of the student. It is certainly not likely to exist among 18-year-old high school graduates.

These realities have significant implications for how educational institutions respond to consumer demand. For profit-maximizing firms in most industries, monitoring consumer preferences is vital, and modifying products in accordance with changing tastes is important for survival. While educational institutions clearly have to be responsive to student preferences in order to survive, if colleges go too far along this path they may be at risk of failing to deliver the product which defines their mission. The familiar questions of whether students should take required courses and whether colleges should continue to offer relatively unpopular programs with intellectual justification are related to this phenomenon. There is some danger in the current market for higher education that more and more institutions will cater to the short-run vocational training demands of students. Although these demands certainly need to be met, and although some institutions may perceive changing in this direction as the only means of survival, in the end, people are not likely to pay the high price of education for simple training. And liberal education with its significant social value could be allowed to disappear because 18-year-olds don't understand its importance.

The job of colleges is to educate students. The fundamental contract between college and student is that faculty and administrators will use their judgment and knowledge to make demands of students that will help them to learn as much as possible. Students cede much of their autonomy and sovereignty to the institutions in which they enroll. They agree to take the courses and meet the academic requirements prescribed by the institution. Students rely on the institution to make many of the decisions about what is best for them. If colleges and universities attempt to cater to the whims of their customers in the way car dealers do, they will be unable to deliver the service that is their reason for being.

In competitive markets, the consumer is supposed to be in charge. If a clothing store doesn't change its fashions to keep up with changing tastes, customers will shop elsewhere. Perhaps a college that fails to offer trendy classes will lose students to competing campuses. This is a much more complicated question than the one about the clothing store. Arguing that student preferences may be cyclical and faddish, and that college enrollments may be affected by this reality, is not the same as arguing that colleges should tailor their curriculum to meet the latest fad. It is entirely reasonable that a college should maintain its archaeology department even if it has very few majors. But that doesn't mean we should fail to understand that the department is likely to cost money and require a transfer of resources from other endeavors. Finding out that the revenues of the college would increase if all required courses were eliminated does not mean there should be radical curriculum reform. But it does mean that the cost of the requirements should be acknowledged and the source of funds to cover those costs should be identified.

Colleges must attract students in order to be able to expose them to the educational opportunities they offer. Ignoring student preferences and willingness to pay is not a viable option. Liberal arts educators may be deeply committed to the idea that this is the form of education that can best prepare people for a changing society and economy. But students have to be open to this idea before they come to college in order to be convinced to enroll in these programs instead of more vocationally oriented training programs. In other words, consumer preferences — and the shaping of consumer preferences — have to play a role in the planning process for educational institutions.

The reality is that a college cannot operate successfully if it does not attract an adequate student population. Elaborate athletic facilities and well-appointed dorm rooms are part of this effort. Balancing the marketing of the institution and the tailoring of its offerings to student demand with the commitment of the faculty and administration to quality education based on their greater knowledge and experience is the challenge.

A Distinctive Enterprise

A standard firm that basic economic models were designed to understand is an enterprise that sells a product to customers in order to make profits. Owners and managers make decisions about how the firm should operate. Other employees are paid to carry out management's decisions. In order to make profits, the firm must produce a product that satisfies customers. Failure to meet customer demands will result in the firm's failure. Firms want to sell their products at the highest possible price to as many buyers as possible.

Most colleges and universities are not making a profit and are operating in order to provide a service. There are no owners and many of the employees — the faculty — participate actively in management decisions.

Several other characteristics of the higher education market differentiate it from many other markets. One is the prevalence of third-party payers. The reality is that despite the increasing prevalence of student loans, most students benefit from some combination of parental contributions, government subsidies, and institutional aid. This means that willingness to pay is not merely a matter of the individual student's attitude toward education. Educational institutions must market themselves to parents as well as students. This may ease the problem that young people don't fully appreciate the benefits, in the case of parents with resources. It also means that many students who themselves would not be willing to pay the full price will attend — clearly a necessity for the viability of many institutions in the current market.

Also significant is the fact that higher education is a product most people purchase only once. No matter how satisfied they are with their college education, the most people can do is recommend the school to family members or friends. Educational institutions are forced to spend considerable resources on consumers who have virtually no chance of being repeat customers. Although some of these expenditures create attributes that improve reputation and draw in future students, others affect only current students.

The selectivity of the admission process at many colleges and universities is also an important distinguishing characteristic. The goal is not to maximize *sales*. The quality of the educational product would likely be diluted by larger classes and less qualified students and the institution's goal is to provide strong educational services — not to maximize revenues. To this end, many colleges and universities enroll students who pay lower prices because they receive institutional grant aid, while they turn away people willing to pay the full sticker price. Unlike other businesses, they turn away potential customers who are able and willing to pay.

Despite the profound differences in mission and operation, colleges and universities operate within a market economy. The fact that most colleges are not-for-profit doesn't mean they have no motivation to operate efficiently. Using more resources than necessary to, for example, run the registrar's office, will mean that there will be less money available to pay faculty. If faculty spend a lot of money going to conferences of questionable value, there will be less money to put into their pension funds. Maximizing the quality of education produced requires efficiency, just as maximizing profits does. Refusing to talk about efficiency is counterproductive.

Sometimes resistance to thinking about the business side of an academic institution is reflected in a failure to consider the concept of opportunity costs. It is difficult for advocates of specific valuable projects to fully weigh the trade-offs involved. It would be better if we had more athletic facilities. State-of-the art computers would improve the classroom experience. Smaller classes are more satisfying than larger ones. Higher salaries will attract better faculty. But we can't do all of the desirable things because we have limited resources. There are trade-offs. The opportunity cost of new computers all over campus may be that faculty salaries will rise more slowly.

Colleges and universities are different from business firms in a variety of ways. They operate for the sake of providing educational opportunities rather than out of primarily financial motivation. The people who buy their services — the students — are an important input into the production process. The quality of education that students receive depends not only on the institution, but also on their own effort and abilities. It also depends on the quality of the other students. Colleges could not provide any reasonable quality of education if they judged each aspect of their operation on its ability to bring in revenues. Nonetheless, in order to continue to be viable, institutions must operate efficiently and limit expenditures to the level of available resources. In the long run, ignoring the bottom line may be as harmful to the educational mission as focusing too narrowly on the bottom line.

The unique characteristics of higher education do not mean that general economic principles do not apply. It may sometimes be useful to think of educational institutions as firms providing a product, of faculty and staff as inputs into a production process, and of students as utility-maximizing consumers. But there is considerable danger in this approach. The issue is not that it demeans the quality or importance of education to think of it as a commodity. Rather, the conditions of production and consumption of higher education are, in some ways, unique. Ignoring this uniqueness can lead to some shortsighted decisions in the supposed interest of efficiency.

Compensation

While faculty salaries usually assure a reasonable middle-class lifestyle, they tend to be lower than salaries in other areas requiring high levels of education and skill. It is not surprising that faculty are frustrated by this reality. The tension that exists on many college campuses about compensation levels is generally not the result of either greed on the part of faculty and staff or ill will on the part of administrators and trustees. Sympathetic as they may be, the holders of the purse strings are all too aware of the major role compensation plays in the overall institutional budget. Increases in salaries and benefits come only at the expense of other campus priorities.

Is there any way to bridge the gap in perspectives on this issue? Although there will always be competing interests, some concrete information may be useful.

Trends in Faculty Salaries

During the 1970s, faculty salaries did not come close to keeping up with inflation. Although salary levels rebounded in the 1980s, the average faculty salary in 1997 was, in inflation-adjusted dollars, almost exactly where it had been in 1970-71. The $52,335 1997-98 salary shown in Table 4 is approximately equal to the $12,710 1970-71 salary shown in the table, converted into 1997 dollars.

Average salaries of full professors — about $69,000 in 1997-98 — can be compared to average salaries for people in the 45 to 54 age bracket: $86,000 for doctorates and $116,000 for professional degrees.[1] The salary gap between academia and other fields is larger for men than for women, since the gender pay gap is lower for academics. Male full professors earn an average of about 13 percent more than female full professors. For year-round, full-time workers between the ages of 45 and 54 with a B.A. or more, men earn about 66 percent more than women.[2]

Faculty salaries vary dramatically from campus to campus. In 1999–2000, the average full professor salary at Harvard was about $129,000 and at Rockefeller University it was close to $130,000. It was over $100,000 at 27 other institutions, not all of which were private. At liberal arts colleges, Wellesley's $95,000 was the highest average salary for full professors. The highest average full professor salary at community colleges was $87,000 and, at 15 of these institutions, it was under $36,000. The average salary for assistant professors at the University of Chicago was twice the average salary for full professors at Bethany College in Kansas.[3] Generally, faculty at doctoral-granting universities earn 50 percent more than those at baccalaureate institutions and those in the Western Pacific and New England regions earn about 30 percent more than those in the South.[4]

In salary discussions, the focus is frequently on how faculty on one campus compare to faculty on another campus. A few words of caution are in order about these comparisons. As is the case with many empirical questions, it is useful to look at the data on faculty salaries sorted in several different ways. The question of whether to

1. Bureau of the Census, op.cit., Table 266.
2. Ibid., Table 758.
3. Denise Magner, "Faculty Salaries Increased 3.7 percent in 1999–2000," *Chronicle of Higher Education*, April 14, 2000.
4. American Association of University Professors, Press Release, www.aaup.org/przrept.htm, March 11, 2000.

Table 4. Salaries of Full-Time Instructional Faculty on Nine-Month Contracts. Salary Trends						
	All faculty	Full	Associate	Assistant	Public 4-yr.	Private 4-yr.
1970-71	$12,710	$17,958	$13,563	$11,176	$13,121	$11,824
1975-76	$16,659	$22,649	$17,065	$13,986	$17,400	$16,116
1980-81	$23,302	$30,753	$23,214	$18,901	$24,373	$22,325
1985-86	$32,392	$42,268	$31,787	$26,277	$34,033	$31,732
1990-91	$42,165	$55,540	$41,414	$34,434	$44,510	$42,224
1995-96	$49,309	$64,540	$47,966	$39,696	$51,172	$50,819
1997-98	$52,335	$68,731	$50,828	$41,830	$54,114	$54,443
Real increase						
1970-75	-6.1%	-9.7%	-9.9%	-10.4%	-5.0%	-2.4%
1975-80	-10.4%	-13.1%	-12.9%	-13.5%	-10.3%	-11.3%
1980-85	+10.7%	+9.4%	+9.0%	+10.7%	+11.2%	+13.1%
1985-90	+5.8%	+6.8%	+5.9%	+6.5%%	+6.3%	+8.1%
1990-95	+1.4%	+0.7%	+0.4%	-0.1%	-0.3%	+4.3%
1995-97	+0.2%	+0.6%	+0.1%	-0.5%	-0.1%	+1.2%

Source: *Digest of Education Statistics, 1999,* Table 339.

compare average salaries across campuses or average salaries within ranks across campuses provides a simple example. Suppose College A and College B have identical salary structures. Average salaries at all ranks are the same. Now College A promotes 10 associate professors to the rank of full professor. College B makes no promotions. Average salaries will go up at College A because of the premium attached to rank. Faculty on College B may complain that they have fallen behind. However, because College A has many new full professors, their average salary for full professors falls, as does the average salary for associate professors, since the most senior members of this group have moved on. So when comparing by ranks, College A finds it has fallen behind College B, and the faculty may complain. A development that really has nothing to do with the generosity of salaries has now created dissatisfaction on both campuses.

Variation in Salaries on Campus

It is not surprising that the combination of the lack of inflation-adjusted growth in earnings and the relatively low level of earnings compared to others with similar levels of education contributes to a sense of dissatisfaction on college campuses. Moreover, salary averages hide some of the issues that are likely to cause tension on campuses. As mentioned above, the gender-based salary disparity has not disappeared, and it is greater in private than in public institutions. The differences are largest at doctoral-granting institutions and for faculty at the rank of full professor. It is not clear what portion of the gap can be explained by differences in discipline and years in rank.

Within institutions, faculty in different fields have very different salary levels. Average salaries in 1998-99 in the field of law averaged $100,549, which is 83

Table 5. Recent Salary Levels (1999–2000).			
Public		**Private independent**	
All	$57,585	All	$66,294
Full	$74,376	Full	$88,356
Associate	$55,348	Associate	$58,972
Assistant	$45,719	Assistant	$48,788
Instructor	$34,422	Instructor	$37,536

Source: *Chronicle of Higher Education*, Facts and Figures, April 4, 2000. Data from American Association of University Professors.

percent higher than the average salary for all disciplines. In chemical engineering, the next highest field, the average is 44 percent above the overall average.[5] Even within the liberal arts there is considerable variation by field in faculty salaries. In 1998-99, in private four-year institutions, professors of English literature earned an average of $49,000 a year, while economists earned $66,000.[6]

Some of the differentials across fields represent real earnings differences, but other factors are also at work. For example, 68 percent of the law faculty are full professors, compared to 35 percent overall and 13 percent in computer information and sciences. Moreover, there are fewer new assistant professors in law — 1 percent in 1998, compared to an average of 5 percent overall and as many as 11 percent in health and medical administrative services.

These disciplinary differences are largely explained by the realities of supply and demand described in Chapter 2. Increased demand for certain types of labor puts upward pressure on wages in those occupations. The decision to pay economists more than philosophers does not imply a judgment that the contribution of one group is any more or less important than the contribution of the other group. But economists have many more employment opportunities outside the academy than philosophers do. In other words, the demand for their services is higher. This means that if the college offers them a low wage, they are likely to choose to work elsewhere. Philosophers with comparable qualifications for teaching and research are not in great demand outside the academy, so more of them will be willing to accept the relatively low salaries offered.

This explanation for salary differentials has nothing to do with equity. The economists are not working harder. They are not necessarily teaching more students or adding more in any way to the output of the institution. This is a situation in which those who focus on what seems fair and those who focus on the dictates of the market are likely to reach different conclusions.

The salary differentials between assistant professors and associate and full professors shown in Table 5 are another area in which dissatisfaction is likely to arise. Again, supply and demand may collide with common notions of equity. In this case, it is the supply side where the differences are clearest. Tenured faculty sometimes receive competing offers from other institutions, but the average senior faculty mem-

---

5. College and University Personnel Association, *National Faculty Salary Survey, 1998-99*, "Executive Summary".
6. *Chronicle of Higher Education*, May 28, 1999.

ber at most institutions has few options but to stay put. The institution does not need to increase full professor wages rapidly in order to prevent the ranks from being depleted.

New assistant professors, on the other hand, are frequently comparing several offers. Although assistant professors are much more likely to be interchangeable than are senior faculty, putting extra dollars into entry-level salaries is more likely to improve the quality of the faculty than putting those dollars into full professor salaries. The institution is more likely to lose young people by offering noncompetitive salaries than to lose those valued members of the community who have been around for years and are central to the functioning of the institution.

Again, the dictates of the market work in a direction which is potentially inconsistent with equity—and with paying people in accordance with their value to the institution. This efficiency argument for a narrowing range of salaries does, however, have limits. If insufficient salary differentials—or insufficient rates of salary growth—damage faculty morale too much, they could seriously affect the quality of the education the institution provides.

Both equity and efficiency considerations should motivate the compensation structure. It may be most efficient to pay generous starting salaries but to hold down salaries for senior faculty who have limited opportunities outside the institution. However, equity considerations may well dictate more generous policies towards senior faculty who provide high levels of campus service and who constitute the core of the academic community.

Nonsalary Compensation

There is no objective answer to the question of what a *fair* level of compensation is. In addressing the issue, however, it is important to consider some factors in addition to salary levels. First, compensation includes not only salary but also benefits. Health care, pensions, life insurance, and other benefits do not appear in salary figures, but they constitute over a quarter of employee compensation and significantly affect standards of living. There is a wide range in the benefits received by college employees, but they are likely to receive benefit packages more generous than those offered in the for-profit sector. Among executive, administrative, and managerial employees in the United States, only 55 percent were included in a pension plan and 67 percent had group health insurance in 1997.[7] It is very important that when comparisons are made, both with alternative forms of employment and across campuses, total compensation levels, not just salary levels, are compared.

Another aspect of compensation that is too easily ignored is what economists call *nonpecuniary benefits*. Some jobs pay higher salaries because they require unpleasant activities. Most people would have to be paid more to be sanitation workers than to work in a clean and pleasant environment. College campuses frequently have high-quality athletic and other types of facilities available to employees. Faculty members, in particular, are likely to be on nine- or ten-month contracts. Although many faculty may be unable to easily supplement their earnings over the summer, they certainly benefit from the flexible academic schedule. They also enjoy regular paid

---

7. *Statistical Abstract of the United States, 1999*, Table 708.

sabbatical leaves, a phenomenon virtually unknown outside the academy. Faculty have an unusual amount of autonomy both in designing their work agendas and in allocating their time. The nature of the academic enterprise would be dramatically transformed if faculty members were required to track their time the way lawyers billing clients must. Probably most notable is that the tenure system provides college faculty with a highly unusual level of job security. In other words, just comparing dollars and cents may give an inaccurate picture of comparative compensation levels.

Staffing Structure

Compensation levels of tenured and tenure-track faculty tell only part of the story. Budget cutting during the 1970s led not only to lower salaries for current faculty but also to a change in the composition of faculty. The trend toward hiring nontenure track and part-time faculty continues on many campuses. In 1970, only 22 percent of instructional faculty were part-time. By 1985, that figure had risen to 36 percent and, by 1997, it was 43 percent[8]. Part-timers are playing a larger role at all types of institutions, from research universities to liberal arts colleges and two-year colleges.

Another cause of tension for faculty is the perception that resources are being diverted away from teaching and research and towards administrative and other functions. As discussed in the preceding chapter, instruction as a percentage of education and general expenditures has fallen over the last two decades. The shift has been largest in private four-year colleges, where the share of expenditures going to instruction has declined by almost one-tenth.[9] Libraries and operation and maintenance of plant have also lost shares of the budget, but all other areas have increased slightly, including research, public service, academic support, and student services.

Faculty are not, however, a declining portion of college and university staff. As Table 6 shows, the percentage of executive/administrative/managerial personnel has not increased, but the proportion of other professional staff has—at the expense of nonprofessional staff. In other words, there is an increase in the status of nonteaching staff on campuses and probably a corresponding increase in compensation. But the idea that there are more and more staff relative to faculty is simply not consistent with the evidence.

Compensation will always be a source of controversy on campus. Faculty salary levels will never compare favorably to earnings in other professions requiring similar amounts of education. Incorporating all of the fringe benefits and nonpecuniary advantages into comparisons of compensation levels is often psychologically difficult, and these advantages don't pay the bills. The combination of the high percentage of college budgets allotted to compensation and the difficulty of increasing productivity (see Chapter 3) makes salary increases a greater strain on campus budgets than is the case in many other industries. Yet failure to adequately compensate faculty and staff will result in an inability to attract and retain high quality educators, undermining the institutional mission. The trend toward part-time faculty

8. *National Center for Education Statistics*, op.cit.(1999) Table 225; *Chronicle of Higher Education, 2000–2001 Almanac*, "Trends in Faculty Employment."
9. Ibid. (1999), Tables 349–353.

Table 6. Changes in the Composition of Staffing Over Time.

	Public		Private	
	1976	1995	1976	1995
Exec/Admin/Man	5%	4%	8%	8%
Faculty	34%	35%	35%	35%
Inst & Research Assts	10%	10%	6%	4%
Other Professionals	10%	17%	9%	18%
Nonprofessional	42%	34%	43%	35%

Source: *Digest of Education Statistics, 1999*, Table 226.

is both a symptom of the problem and an omen of the potential dangers. A clear understanding of opportunity costs — of what is sacrificed in all the choices made about budgets — is vital for the future of educational institutions.

Tenure

Questions from the public, from state legislatures, and from boards of trustees about the practice of faculty tenure are increasingly common and increasingly critical. Proposals have been made in several states to eliminate tenure at public colleges. The end of mandatory retirement has made concerns about the system more prominent. Because it is difficult to find other industries in which employees have the level of job security granted to tenured faculty, it is not surprising that the wisdom of the system is not obvious to all observers. Yet there is probably no other subject that angers faculty more. Economic analysis cannot shed much light on the fundamental argument for tenure, which is the assurance of academic freedom. Nonetheless, an understanding of the academic labor market and how it is affected by the tenure system is a critical underpinning for any discussion of tenure. Given the weight of compensation in college and university budgets, it is impossible to expect that those responsible for the bottom line will not insist that the financial implications of the system be taken into account.

Job Security

There are a variety of realities not related to academic freedom or ideology that might cause colleges and universities to lay off some number of senior-level faculty members in the absence of a tenure system. Like any business, colleges and universities face fluctuations in the demand for their product. Changing demographics and economic conditions can have a dramatic effect on the number of applications a college receives. It is possible that in the absence of tenure, a significant number of faculty would lose their jobs during periods of low enrollment. On most college campuses, this is a startling idea.

Of course, in other industries, layoffs are an accepted reality. This makes it difficult for outsiders to understand why academics should be so protected from market forces. However, headlines about massive layoffs may bias perceptions of corporate personnel practices. The costs of turnover, which include search and training processes, are quite high. Among male workers between the ages of 45 and 54, 28 percent have been with their current employer for over 20 years and another 22 percent have over 10 years of tenure with their current employer.[10] Since a significant percentage of job changes are voluntary, it is clear that most workers are not involuntarily separated from their firms. The cost to firms of turnover among highly trained employees is particularly high and the length of job tenure is positively correlated with level of education. The median length of time people between the ages of 55 and 64 who have doctoral or professional degrees have been with their current employer is about 15 years.[11]

The particularly specialized training of college and university faculty creates special circumstances in their labor market. The difficulty of applying the skill set of an art history professor to any other type of job makes it quite reasonable that faculty are willing to sacrifice some current earnings in exchange for job security.

There are also some strong efficiency arguments for continuous employment from the perspective of the institution. Experience and attachment to the institution have a significant impact on an individual's contribution. Faculty members do not just teach courses. They know the particular students at their schools and they work closely with their colleagues in a variety of ways. There is relatively little turnover in most college faculties. A dramatic change in the employment relationships could change that pattern, diminishing the collaborative nature of the educational environment.

In other industries, where there is usually more of a hierarchy and more variety in the jobs available to individual employees, the most competent employees are likely to be promoted frequently. Those whose performance is more mediocre may stay put or be moved to jobs with less responsibility. About a quarter of the employees between the ages of 30 and 40 were promoted between 1995 and 1997, and 36 percent of male college graduates were promoted during this time period.[12] This sort of job change is rarely available to academics. Tenure, with its stringent one-time evaluation process, is a system much more suited to academia than to other industries.[13]

Productivity

Many of the arguments against tenure are based on the idea that there is no way to enforce continuing productivity among tenured faculty. Economic theories of the labor market are generally based on the idea that employers are unwilling to pay workers more than the amount their productivity contributes to the enterprise. A profit-making organization cannot survive if it is losing money because of unproductive employees. But colleges are not profit-making organizations. And on many campuses, it is possible to find some number of tenured faculty who do not pull their weight. This inefficiency is seen by some as an argument for abandoning the tenure system.

---

10. *Statistical Abstract of the United States, 1999*, Table 670.
11. Bureau of Labor Statistics,http://BLS.gov/news.release/tenure.t02.htm.
12. Bureau of Labor Statistics,http://BLS.gov/news.release/tenure.t02.htm.
13. See Michael McPherson, Morton Schapiro, and Gordon Winston, *Paying the Piper*, for a more detailed discussion of this issue.

One interesting aspect of the higher education industry is that measuring productivity is not clear-cut. If a professor teaches poorly but students continue to register for her classes out of necessity, how is the decline in productivity observed? If too many faculty are in this category, enrollments will surely decline. But students who take these courses still get their credits and graduate, so a few burned-out faculty may not, in fact, have a measurable economic effect on the institution.

Moreover, it is not at all clear that tenure has a negative impact on faculty productivity. By allowing them the luxury of focusing on their role in a particular institution, rather than on more widely marketable, less institution-specific activities, tenure has a tendency to fosters an unusually engaged and dedicated employee community. A 1998 study of the relationship between tenure and faculty productivity provided evidence that tenured faculty are not less productive than untenured faculty. One finding is that while tenured faculty tend to teach less, they tend to spend more time on administrative tasks.[14]

Another interesting perspective on the productivity impact of tenure comes from the theory of x-efficiency in labor markets. Theorists have long recognized that maximum productivity may not result from maximum exposure to market forces. Workers who are satisfied, who feel appreciated, and who enjoy a comfortable, rewarding work environment are likely to be more productive than those who are treated poorly and are frustrated with their circumstances. Higher wages and better working conditions may actually directly increase worker productivity. Tenure and the accompanying sense of belonging in an institution are likely to have a strong positive effect on faculty commitment to their teaching, their professional work, and their service to the college or university community. In the absence of tenure, faculty focus would be much more on professional accomplishments in the interest of mobility than on activities that directly affect the students and the rest of the college community.

Despite the difficulty of defining and measuring productivity for faculty, the academy has developed an elaborate and thorough evaluation process for tenure. Most institutions put considerable resources into evaluating individual faculty members in their sixth year of employment. The probability that a faculty member whose performance is adequate but not spectacular will lose his or her job after the probationary period is significantly greater than the probability that an employee with a similar level of performance in another industry would be fired. It may well also be significantly higher than it would be under any sort of contract system that might replace tenure. At least one study has found that institutions without tenure have no more turnover than those with tenure.[15] The lifetime character of the tenure contract makes the scrutiny applied much more intense.

The tenure system does appear to decrease mobility at higher levels in the academic labor market. In the corporate world, it is not uncommon for management level personnel to move from one company to another. Searches for upper-level employees are common because vacancies arise for a variety of reasons. Theoretical models of labor markets that describe the demanders of labor as constantly finding the most productive workers at the lowest possible cost are clearly unrealistic. Still,

14. James S. Antony and Joyce S. Raveling, "A Comparative Analysis of Tenure and Faculty Productivity," ERIC #ED427598, 1998; and National Center for Education Statistics, *The Condition of Education, 2000*, Section 5.
15. Richard Chait, "The Future of Academic Tenure," *AGB Priorities*, Number 3, Spring 1995.

profit-making companies must, of necessity, monitor productivity levels and replace workers who do not carry their weight.

The tenure system interferes with this process. We wait for unproductive workers to retire. This means that there are fewer openings for senior-level faculty. Because of this, senior faculty are in a weaker bargaining position with respect to compensation. It is reasonable to believe that the differential in salaries across ranks is smaller than it would be in the absence of a tenure system. Tenured faculty get part of their compensation in the form of job security and the paucity of job options for senior faculty means the salary increases need not be particularly steep.

Alternative Arrangements

As discussed above, in recent years an increasing number of faculty are part-time or adjunct. This development is of considerable concern to faculty interested in preserving tenure. It is a natural market response to the institution of tenure, however. In the interest of keeping compensation costs down and of avoiding long-term commitments in an uncertain, competitive environment, institutions are finding ways to hire people to whom they are not required to make a lifetime commitment. It can certainly be argued that the inflexibility of the tenure system leaves the administration no choice but to find alternative employment arrangements. That said, there is no doubt that these arrangements pose a threat both to the practice of tenure and to the quality of the educational environment as traditionally defined.

The percentage of full-time instructional faculty with tenure is higher at public institutions than at private institutions, while private universities have more of their full-time faculty on nontenure track appointments. Overall, as Table 7 shows, the proportion of full-time faculty members with tenure in 1993 was 51 percent, about the same as in 1975. However, the proportion who were nontenure track — as opposed to being in the probationary period — rose from 19 to 28 percent over this period of time.[16] The fact that a significantly smaller proportion of the instructional faculty are fulltime means that tenure ratios have not held constant in any meaningful sense.

Table 7. Faculty Status.	1975	1993		1975	1993
Full-time faculty	56%	49%	**All faculty**		
% Tenured	52%	51%	% Tenured	29%	25%
% Probationary	29%	21%	% Probationary	16%	10%
% Nontenure Track	19%	28%	% Nontenure Track	10%	14%
			% Part-Time.	24%	33%
			% Grad Asst.	20%	18%

Source: *AAUP Footnotes*, www.aaup.org/fnebta3.htm, 1997, Table 3.

16. National Center for Education Statistics, "Instructional Faculty and Staff in Higher Education Institutions: Fall 1987 and Fall 1992," 1993 National Study of Postsecondary Faculty, Statistical Analysis Report, July 1997; Courteney Leatherman, "Growth in Positions Off the Tenure Track Is a Trend That's Here to Stay, Study Finds," *Chronicle of Higher Education*, April 9, 1999.

The trend toward part-time and adjunct faculty may have a variety of explanations. The dramatic move to part-time in the 1970s reflects both the growth in community colleges and the financial strain that caused salaries to decline. But the perception of limited staffing flexibility in the face of economic and enrollment fluctuations is a powerful motivation behind the search for alternative employment arrangements.

Some prominent institutions now give faculty a choice of a tenure track or a long-term rolling contract with a salary premium. Other institutions provide more frequent sabbaticals to those who opt out of the tenure system. There is evidence that a clear majority of faculty choose these nontenure options.[17] A number of lesser known colleges and universities have simply eliminated tenure as an option.

In addition to the increasing reliance on part-time and adjunct faculty, a variety of modifications to traditional faculty employment patterns are developing. These changes are rooted in concern over the cost and inflexibility of tenure. But the question of whether the tenure system increases the cost of compensation for institutions is not straightforward. On one hand, colleges and universities are not free to replace higher-paid senior faculty with lower-paid junior faculty at will or even in order to increase the quality of education offered. On the other hand, faculty salaries are surely lower than they would be in a labor market characterized by more competition among institutions. The relatively high salaries of the small number of "stars" in academia, who do in fact experience competitive bidding for their services, provide some clues about the direction in which a free market might lead. Simple statements about how we can't afford the tenure system may not be well informed. On the other hand, a failure to understand the very significant role tenure plays in the compensation of faculty can make faculty feel underrewarded.

The growing prevalence of nontenure track positions on campuses with entrenched tenure systems and the increase in institutions abandoning the system altogether raise the question of whether tenure will be gradually eroded without a clear direction or sense of the potential damage.

Avoiding the debate about tenure could have serious negative results. Failure to face the labor market implications of tenure head on may cause the system to wither without any conscious decisions to repeal it. An open dialogue on the subject with the possibility of some modifications carefully designed with the interests of academic freedom and faculty autonomy at the core may be preferable to the gradual undermining of the system most faculty view as fundamental to their professional work.

Financial Aid: Need-Based Versus Merit-Based

Because neither family income nor government-funded student aid has kept up with the rate of increase in college costs, institutional aid has become much more important in making college affordable. Particularly dramatic is the increasing percentage of the budget being devoted to scholarships and fellowships at private four-year colleges. Grants have increased from 4 percent to between 5 and 6 percent of education

17. Denise Magner, "Tenure Re-examined," *Chronicle of Higher Education*, March 3, 1995, and Louis Lataif, "A Realistic Alternative to Traditional Tenure," *Chronicle of Higher Education*, June 26, 1998.

and general expenses in the public sector and from 8 to 11 percent in private universities, but from 10 to 18 percent in private four-year colleges.[18]

Debates about the criteria on which the allocation of aid dollars should be based are heated, both on college campuses and in the public policy arena. In recent years, federal and state governments, as well as many colleges and universities—both public and private—have engaged in new ways of providing financial aid to students. In the late 1980s and the 1990s, with increased competition for qualified students and with growing public pressure to reduce the strain on middle-class families struggling to pay for college, more and more aid dollars from all sources became non-need based. Between 1983-84 and 1991-92, the portion of aid at public institutions based on criteria other than need rose from 44 to 56 percent, and on private campuses, where institutional dollars are more plentiful, it rose from 17 to 21 percent.[19] Although exact figures are not available, the trend has continued. The balance has not tipped as much at the most selective colleges as it has at those schools struggling to fill their seats or to attract higher quality students.

As colleges and universities are providing more grants based on academic qualifications (in addition to athletic skills, diversity factors, and other student traits), states are following Georgia's lead in designing scholarship programs for students with relatively high GPAs. This trend towards merit-based aid is significant in terms of demographics, since non-need based aid goes disproportionately to white students, with Asian, black, and Hispanic students getting a smaller share of the funds.[20] Because academic credentials tend to be positively correlated with family income, these programs do not target low-income students.

As detailed in Chapter 1, federal need-based financial aid continues to increase, although not rapidly enough to keep up with college costs for low-income students. Federal subsidies to college students have, instead, been expanded to include tax credits for tuition payments. Of the approximately $3.5 billion dollars in tax credits for college expenses claimed on 1999 tax returns, about half came from returns with income exceeding $50,000. Only 13 percent of the credits went to families with incomes below $20,000.[21] The federal move towards tax-based aid policies reinforces the state and institutional policies redirecting aid away from the students who have the most difficulty paying for college.

Each campus must study its situation carefully and reach its own conclusions about the appropriate balance between need-based and merit-based aid. However, like other controversial topics, this issue can be more effectively addressed against a background of accurate information and a sound analytical framework.

---

18. National Center for Education Statistics, op.cit., Tables 349-353.

19. Michael McPherson and Morton Schapiro, *The Student Aid Game* (Princeton: Princeton University Press, 1998), p. 117.

20. Ibid., p. 124.

21. Sara Hebel, "In Year 2 of Tuition Tax Credits, Colleges Cope Better, But Still Complain," *Chronicle of Higher Education*, April 12, 2000.

Ability to Pay Versus Willingness to Pay

As discussed in Chapters 2 and 3, with financial aid programs different students pay different prices for the same educational experience on the same college campus. Charging consumers different prices for the same product is price discrimination. Straightforward economic theory explains price discrimination in terms of the different demand curves of different consumers. Some people are willing and able to pay a higher price than others for the same product. In most markets, we don't worry much about the difference between willingness to pay and ability to pay. All that matters is effective demand—the demand for a product backed up by the dollars to pay for it. However, when the good or service in question is one to which society values access for all individuals, the distinction is very important.

Need-based financial aid systems are designed to allow those who cannot enroll because of financial constraints to attend. They are designed to tackle the problem of ability to pay. They are not designed to draw in students who have the ability to pay but who don't want the education the school can offer enough to make them willing to pay. For some colleges and universities, these price discounts to selected students are necessary to assure adequate enrollments. At other institutions— generally those that are more affluent and more selective—financial aid is really a discretionary expenditure. These colleges and universities are choosing to use funds to increase the diversity of the student body and to provide access to education to a broader group of students.

Skyrocketing tuition levels, increased competition among institutions for students, and the pervasiveness of explicit subsidies to students have combined to make families with ample resources less willing to pay institutions' sticker prices. They are more likely to try to bargain, asking one school to beat the offer they have received from another school. They are also more likely to have a sense of entitlement, believing it is someone else's responsibility to shoulder at least part of the financial burden of higher education. Many colleges and universities have found themselves diverting aid dollars to potential students based on a lack of willingness to pay, rather than on a lack of ability to pay.

Of course, both willingness and ability to pay must be present for a student to enroll. However, inadequate ability to pay cannot be overcome without providing subsidies. In contrast, colleges, like other producers, have other means for affecting willingness to pay. While traditional advertising is not common in higher education, attractive promotional materials and aggressive marketing are increasingly visible. And, of course, colleges can improve their educational offerings and their facilities in an effort to draw students to their institutions.

The Need-Based Aid System

The need-based aid system is complicated and the appearance of some inequities surely diminishes support for it. It is always possible to find someone who has a need-based grant who seems to be living quite well. And there are certainly many people struggling to scrape together tuition dollars who have been denied need-based aid. Some background about the system may be useful.

The federal need-based financial aid system consists of a combination of grants, loans, and work assistance. The allocation of these funds is based on a formula legislated by Congress and known as the Federal Methodology. It is based on the annual income of custodial parents and of students. Although some other information is collected in the application process, the details of financial circumstances are, by and large, not taken into account.

Colleges that have their own funds to devote to student aid frequently use a more complicated formula that has the disadvantage of requiring more information and being more difficult to understand, but the advantage of being able to more accurately distinguish among families and students with different capacities to pay. Some colleges use their own formulas, but many rely, at least to some extent, on the Institutional Methodology developed and maintained by the College Board. This formula considers both the income and the assets of parents and students in determining ability to pay. Like the federal formula, this formula defines need as the difference between the cost of attending a particular college and the amount the student and his or her family are deemed able to pay.

Like any formula, the need-based financial aid formulas have arbitrary elements. They cannot sort families out perfectly. There is not one precise answer to the question of how much anyone can afford for college. Still, financial aid offices work hard to assure that need is measured accurately and that aid dollars are allocated to those who need them most.

Price Competition

Increasingly, financial aid is viewed not only as a tool to increase access to higher education and to provide broader institutional choice to students, but also as an enrollment management tool for colleges and universities. Giving aid awards to students who would enroll without them means forgoing revenue unnecessarily and losing some other students who might be induced by grant aid to enroll. In other words, prudent financial management dictates the strategic use of financial aid funds.

This idea opens the door to a variety of aid allocation practices. There is no easy answer to the balancing act now required in using institutional grant dollars to meet the multiple goals of increasing access and diversity, filling the class with the highest quality students possible, and assuring financial stability. Many colleges and universities have found merit-based scholarships to be an effective tool for improving the academic profile of the student body or for increasing enrollments. The potential effectiveness of such as strategy on a particular campus depends on a variety of factors, including selectivity, the percentage of the applicant pool currently being accepted, and the percentage of those accepted who enroll. The number of students currently receiving institutional grant aid and the discount rate—the percentage of gross tuition revenues being offered as grant aid—are also very relevant.

Whatever its short-term effectiveness, if this competitive strategy continues to become more prevalent, it is unlikely to have a positive effect on higher education in the long term. In the 1980s, financial aid practices were characterized by cooperation among institutions attempting to reduce the impact of financial circumstances on college choice. In the 1990s, the antitrust case brought by the Justice Department against many private institutions, combined with the declining college-aged population and financial constraints, contributed to reduced cooperation and increased competition. Financial aid is increasingly being used as a competitive tool to attract students to particular institutions. This competition may be a major destructive force in higher education in the long run.

Like any firms engaged in price competition, colleges that lower their prices for desirable students find that their competitors are forced to follow suit. This generates a cycle of price cutting for students with particular characteristics — high SAT® scores, particular racial backgrounds, or athletes, for example. This price cutting cannot significantly increase the overall supply of students in these categories. As more and more institutional aid dollars are devoted to these students, fewer resources will be available for other priorities, including need-based aid for qualified students who cannot afford to enroll. Higher education economists are watching this process with concern and predicting potentially serious results for higher education as an industry. Although no individual institution can solve this problem on its own, an awareness of the interaction between short-term strategies and long-term outcomes should inform campus discussions.

Applying Economic Principles to Other Issues

The issues discussed in this chapter are just a few examples of topics that frequently create tensions on college campuses. There are many other problems that can benefit from a similar form of discourse. Very few campus issues should be viewed as purely economic in nature. College finances are supportive of the central educational mission, not the primary motivating factor. Nonetheless, the understanding and application of basic economic concepts can frequently raise the level of debate on campus. Probably most important is that the concept of opportunity cost be part of conversations about campus priorities. No matter what the endeavor in question, it will require resources that could be used for other purposes. The issues discussed in this chapter are no exception. Compensation levels cannot be increased without either increasing revenues or reducing expenditures in another area. Conscious choices about sacrificing some goals in the interest of higher priorities are always preferable to a narrow focus on a particular project.

The concepts of equity and efficiency also have a place in most decisions. Sometimes these considerations will reinforce each other. It may be both equitable and efficient to give price discounts to qualified students who cannot otherwise afford to enroll. It may be both equitable and efficient to assure that all employees have access to adequate health care. But in other cases, there may be trade-offs between the two values, as is frequently the case in setting salary differentials by ranks. An open and honest conversation about the costs and benefits of privileging one goal over the other in solving any particular problem is a prerequisite to cooperative decision making rooted in mutual trust and respect.

Questions for Discussion

Many campus issues can benefit from a dialogue grounded in a thoughtful analysis of the issues, combining a strong commitment to the fundamental educational mission of the institution with a clear view of economic principles and financial realities. The following questions may serve as a starting point for campus discussions.

1. Have any recent cost-cutting innovations at your college or university had a significant negative effect on the quality of education provided to students? How might the changes be modified to remedy the situation?

2. Have enrollments at your institution been steady over time? What would be the advantages and disadvantages of either increasing or decreasing the size of the student body?

3. What portion of the faculty on your campus are part-time? How many full-time faculty are nontenure track? Have these proportions increased over time? Why? What has the impact been?

4. How much do faculty salaries on your campus vary by field? Are there significant gender-based salary differences? How does your institution compare faculty salaries to salaries at other colleges and universities?

5. What criteria does your college or university use to allocate financial aid? Have these criteria changed significantly in recent years? Do you have need-blind admission, or do an individual's financial circumstances play a role in admission decisions? Does your school meet the financial need of accepted candidates? What are the implications of these policies?

6. Is your institution involved in outsourcing? Does it contract out for the bookstore, dining services, technology, maintenance services, or other services? What are the pros and cons of this approach? What are the equity and efficiency considerations related to outsourcing decisions?

7. Is your college or university involved in any distance learning projects? Are these efforts designed to be profitmaking? Will they substitute for existing educational methods or will they broaden the constituency or the opportunities available at the institution?

8. How are decisions about investments in technology being made on your campus? Has technology increased productivity and reduced costs, or does it actually tend to increase the cost of existing activities? What are the arguments for updating technology more rapidly? More slowly?

9. Are there any for-profit enterprises on your campus? What would be the reaction if your institution pursued this course? What are alternative sources for increased revenues to support the academic program?

10. Can you think of any areas on campus where economies of scale could be more fully exploited? Are there situations in which bringing together larger groups would improve, or at least not dilute, quality? Are there areas on campus where breaking efforts down into smaller pieces would improve quality?

11. Might there be economies of scope involved in any of the new initiatives currently under discussion? Are resources available on campus that could be more fully exploited by engaging in activities related to those already being undertaken?

12. Are you aware of the development of the for-profit sector in higher education? In what ways might your institution be threatened by the spread of for-profit training programs and distance learning opportunities?

13. If you could choose one new program or project to introduce on your campus, or one endeavor to strengthen significantly, what would it be? What would the *opportunity cost* be? Where can resources be released?

14. Are there any areas in which your institution prides itself on efficient practices? In what ways might efficiency be increased on your campus? Are there policies and practices that are generally praised for their equity? Is there any consensus on notable inequities?

AUTHOR BIOGRAPHY

Sandy Baum is professor of Economics at Skidmore College, where she has served as chair of the Department of Economics, assistant to the dean of the Faculty for Diversity and Affirmative Action, and director of the Law and Society Program. She is an active participant in all aspects of faculty governance. She graduated from Bryn Mawr College in 1972 with a major in sociology and received her Ph.D. in economics from Columbia University in 1981. Before coming to Skidmore, she taught at Northeastern University and Wellesley College.

Dr. Baum's primary area of research is higher education economics. She has written on financial aid policy, the distribution of subsidies to college students, merit aid, college savings plans, student debt and other aspects of college finance. She has published articles on these topics in numerous journals in both economics and higher education, in addition to contributing to several books. She has spoken to a wide variety of audiences on topics relating to student aid and college finance.

Dr. Baum has served as a consulting economist for the College Board's Financial Aid Standards and Services Committee since 1988. Her *Primer on Economics for Financial Aid Professionals* was published jointly by NASFAA and the College Board in 1996.